First International Workshop on Language Cognition and Computational Models (LCCM-2018)

Santa Fe, New Mexico, USA
20 August 2018

ISBN: 978-1-5108-6907-3

Printed by Curran Associates, Inc. (2018)

For permission requests, please contact the Association for Computational Linguistics
at the address below.

Association for Computational Linguistics
209 N. Eighth Street
Stroudsburg, Pennsylvania 18360

Phone: 1-570-476-8006
Fax: 1-570-476-0860

acl@aclweb.org

Additional copies of this publication are available from:

Curran Associates, Inc.
57 Morehouse Lane
Red Hook, NY 12571 USA
Phone: 845-758-0400
Fax: 845-758-2633
Email: curran@proceedings.com
Web: www.proceedings.com

COLING 2018

**The 27th International Conference
on Computational Linguistics**

**Proceedings of the First International Workshop on Language
Cognition and Computational Models (LCCM-2018)**

August 20, 2018
Santa Fe, New Mexico, USA

Introduction

Welcome to the COLING-2018 Workshop on Language, Cognition and Computational Models!

Language as a communication tool is one of the key attributes of human society. It is also what distinguishes human communication from most of the other species. Language is, arguably, also what shapes our view of the world. However, language is a complex and intricate tool developed and is continuously evolving over thousands of years, influenced by usage, demographics, and socio-cultural factors. The study of language communication, comprehension and it's complex interaction with thought is a rapidly expanding multi-disciplinary and challenging field of research. This growth comes from both its domain and its interdisciplinary nature that confluences cognitive science, computer science, neuroscience, linguistics, psycholinguistics, psychology and many other fields. The development of increasingly sophisticated tools are making it possible to studying different brain activities. A plethora of works have been done studying the representation, organization and processing of language in the human mind. Despite such huge efforts, a coherent picture is yet to emerge. We are yet to go a long-way to develop holistic computational models and make up for the scarcity of corpora in variety of languages.

In addition, each language possess a beauty and uniqueness of its own, and demands a customized approach to understand its intricate relationship with speakers. We especially, encourage works in low resourced and less studied languages and our workshop aims to provide a suitable platform to those less articulated voices.

The goal of this workshop is to bring together researchers working in the field of linguistics, cognitive science, computer science and the intersection of these areas, together and provide a venue for the multidisciplinary discussion of theoretical and practical research for computational models of language and cognition. This knowledge does not only answer one of the primary aspects of cognitive science, but also is useful for designing better NLP systems based on the understood principles. The focus centers around recent advances on cognitively motivated computational models for language representation, organization, processing, acquisition, comprehension and evolution. Given the lack of large standardized corpora for this area of research, we are also interested in developing public data sets for the area and various languages..

Organizers

Manjira Sinha, Accenture AI Labs, India: is associate principal artificial intelligence at Accenture AI Labs. Prior to that she was a research scientist in the Text and Graph Analytics research group at Conduent Labs India (formerly known as Xerox Research Centre India) for 3 years. She is currently working in NLP for Healthcare. She has also worked on cross-domain Text categorization, Social Media analysis for Urban Informatics, Knowledge Extraction, and Quality Analysis for Call center Interactions. Manjira has a Ph.D. in Computer Science from the Indian Institute of Technology Kharagpur. She is also visiting faculty in Indian Institute of Information Technology Kalyani. Her areas of interest include Language Comprehension and Psycholinguistics, Natural Language Processing, Assistive Technology and Human Computer Interaction.

https://www.linkedin.com/in/manjira-sinha-8554b157/

Tirthankar Dasgupta, Innovation Labs, Tata Consultancy Services Limited, India: is a research scientist at Innovation Labs, Tata Consultancy Services Ltd., India in the Text Analytics and Web Intelligence group. He holds a Ph.D. in computer science from Indian Institute of Technology, Kharagpur. His research interests span natural language processing, computational psycholinguistics, machine learning and human computer interaction. He has organized a number of workshops in the area of assistive technology and natural language processing. He is also an active organizing member and regional coordinator of Panini Linguistic Olympiad in India. He was an organizing member of International Linguistic Olympiad 2016 in India.

https://www.linkedin.com/in/tirthankar-dasgupta-89b0551/

Programme Committee

Narayanan Srinivasan, Centre of Behavioural and Cognitive Sciences , University of Allahabad
Monojit Choudhury, Microsoft Research India
Pabitra Mitra, Indian Institute of Technology Kharagpur (IIT), India
Dipti Mishra Sharma, International Institute of Information Technology Hyderabad (IIIT-H), India
Ayesha Kidwai, Jawaharlal Nehru University, India
Jiaul Paik, Indian Institute of Technology Kharagpur (IIT), India
Rajlakshmi Guha, Indian Institute of Technology Kharagpur (IIT), India.
Priyanka Sinha, TCS Innovation Labs, India
Lipika Dey, TCS Innovation Labs
Kalika Bali, Microsoft Research, India
Amitava Das, IIIT Sri City
Sunandan Chakraborty, New York University
Sandya Mannarswamy, Conduent Labs India
Vaishna Narang, Jawaharlal Nehru University, India
Rupsa Saha, TCS Innovation Labs, India
Moumita Saha, TCS Innovation Labs, India
Bornini Lahiri, Jadavpur University, India Ritesh Kumar, Bhim Rao Ambedkar University, India
Dripta Piplai, IIT Kharagpur

Table of Contents

Conference Program

A Compositional Bayesian Semantics for Natural Language

Jean-Philippe Bernardy   Rasmus Blanck   Stergios Chatzikyriakidis   Shalom Lappin
University of Gothenburg
`firstname.lastname@gu.se`

Abstract

We propose a compositional Bayesian semantics that interprets declarative sentences in a natural language by assigning them probability conditions. These are conditional probabilities that estimate the likelihood that a competent speaker would endorse an assertion, given certain hypotheses. Our semantics is implemented in a functional programming language. It estimates the marginal probability of a sentence through Markov Chain Monte Carlo (MCMC) sampling of objects in vector space models satisfying specified hypotheses. We apply our semantics to examples with several predicates and generalised quantifiers, including higher-order quantifiers. It captures the vagueness of predication (both gradable and non-gradable), without positing a precise boundary for classifier application. We present a basic account of semantic learning based on our semantic system. We compare our proposal to other current theories of probabilistic semantics, and we show that it offers several important advantages over these accounts.

1 Introduction

In classical model theoretic semantics (Montague 1974; Dowty, Wall, and Peters 1981; Barwise and Cooper 1981) the interpretation of a declarative sentence is given as a set of truth conditions with Boolean values. This excludes vagueness from semantic interpretation, and it does not provide a natural framework for explaining semantic learning. Indeed, semantic learning involves the acquisition of classifiers (predicates), which seems to require probabilistic learning.[1]

Recently several theories of probabilistic semantics for natural language have been proposed to accommodate both phenomena (van Eijck and Lappin 2012; Cooper et al. 2014; Cooper et al. 2015; Goodman and Lassiter 2015; Lassiter 2015; Lassiter and Goodman 2017; Sutton 2017). These accounts offer interesting ways of expressing vagueness, and suggestive approaches to semantic learning. They also suffer from a number of serious shortcomings, some of which we briefly discuss in Section 4.

In this paper we propose a compositional Bayesian semantics for natural language in which we assign probability rather than truth conditions to declarative sentences. We estimate the conditional probability of a sentence as the likelihood that an idealised competent speaker of the language would accept the assertion that the sentence expresses, given fixed interpretations of generalised quantifiers and certain other terms, and a set of specified hypotheses, $p_S(A \mid H)$. S is a competent speaker of the language, A is the assertion that the sentence expresses, and H is the set of hypotheses on which we are conditioning the likelihood that S will endorse A. On this approach assessing the probability of a sentence in the circumstances defined by the hypotheses is an instance of evaluating the application of a classifier acquired through supervised learning, to a new argument (set of arguments).

Our semantics interprets sentences as probabilistic programs (Borgström et al. 2013). Section 2 gives a detailed description of our implementation. It involves encoding objects and properties as vectors in vector space models. Our system uses Markov Chain Monte Carlo (MCMC) sampling, as implemented

---

[1]See (Clark and Lappin 2011) for a discussion of computational learning and probabilistic learning models for natural language.

Proceedings of the First International Workshop on Language Cognition and Computational Models, pages 1–10
Santa Fe, New Mexico, United States, August 20, 2018.
https://doi.org/10.18653/v1/P17

in WebPPL (Goodman and Stuhlmüller 2014), a lightweight version of Church (Goodman et al. 2008), and it estimates the marginal probabilities of predications and quantified sentences relative to the models satisfying the constraints of an asserted set of hypotheses ($p_S(A \mid H)$).

We give examples of inferences involving several generalised quantifiers, including higher-order quantifiers (in the sense of Barwise and Cooper (1981)) like *most*. Our semantics uses the same vector space models and sampling mechanism to express both the vagueness of gradable predicates, like *tall*, and of ordinary property terms, such as *red* and *chair*.

Our semantic framework does not require extensive lexically specified content or pragmatic knowledge statements to estimate the parameters of our vector space models. It also does not posit boundary values (hard coded or contextually specified) for the application of a predicate to an argument.

The system that we describe here is a prototype that offers a proof of concept for our approach. A robust, wide coverage version of this system will be useful for a variety of tasks. Three examples are as follows.

First, we intend to encode both semantic and real world knowledge as priors in our models. These will sustain probabilistic inferencing that will support text understanding and question answering in a way analogous to that in which Bayesian Networks are used for inference and knowledge representation in restricted domains. Second, we envisage an integration of visual and other non-linguistic vector representations into our models. This will facilitate the evaluation of candidate descriptions of images and scenes. It will also allow us to assess the relative accuracy of statements concerning these scenes. Finally, our system could be used as a filter on machine translation. Source and target sentences are expected to share the same probability values for the same models. The success which our framework achieves in these applications will provide criteria for evaluating it.

In Section 3 we present an outline of our implemented system for semantic learning, that extends our compositional semantics to the probabilistic acquisition of classifiers.

In Section 4 we compare our system to recent work in probabilistic semantics.

Finally, in Section 5 we state the main conclusions of our research, and we indicate the issues that we will address in future work.

2   An Implemented Probabilistic Semantics

Our semantics draws inspiration from (i) Montague semantics, (ii) vector space models, and (iii) Bayesian inference. Additionally, the implementation is guided by programming language theory. At the front-end we rely on a precise semantics for probabilistic programming, provided by Borgström et al., using their effect system to make explicit the sampling of parameters and observations. At the backend, we estimate probabilities using MCMC sampling, as described by Goodman et al. (2008). The implementation is encoded as a Haskell library. It makes effects explicit using a monadic system, with calls into Goodman's WebPPL language for probability approximation.[2]

Following Montague, our semantics assumes an assignment from syntactic categories to types. These assignments are given in Haskell as follows:

```
type Pred = Ind → Prop
type Measure = Ind → Scalar
type AP = Measure
type CN = Ind → Prop
type VP = Ind → Prop
type NP = VP → Prop
type Quant = CN → NP
```

While Montague leaves individuals *Ind* as an abstract type, we give it a concrete definition. We represent individuals as vectors, and propositions as (probabilistic) Booleans. Additionally, adjectival phrases are treated as scalars, and so they are expressed by a real number.

---

[2]The code for our system is available at `https://github.com/GU-CLASP/CompositionalBayesianSemantics`.

Crucially, the evaluation of every expression is probabilistic. The meaning of each expression in our semantic domain is itself a probability distribution, whose value can be computed symbolically using the rules provided by Borgström et al. (2013), or approximated with a tool such as WebPPL.

2.1 Individuals and Predicates

We can illustrate these concepts by a simple example, written in Haskell syntax, using our front end.

```
modelSimplest = do
    p ← newPred
    x ← newInd
    return (p x)
```

The function *modelSimplest* declares a predicate p and an individual x, and probabilistically evaluates the proposition "x satisfies p". Note that "newPred" and "newInd" have the *effect* of sampling over their respective distribution (we clarify those shortly), and so have monadic types. In the absence of further information, an arbitrary predicate has an even chance to hold of an arbitrary individual. Running the model, using our implementation, gives the following approximate result:

```
false : 0.544     true : 0.456
```

The distribution of individuals is a multi-variate normal distribution of dimension k, with a zero mean vector and a unit covariance matrix, and where k is a hyperparameter of the system.

```
newInd = newVector
newVector = mapM (uncurry sampleGaussian) (replicate k (0, 1))
```

Predicates are parameterised by a bias b and a vector d, given by normalizing a vector sampled in the same multi-variate normal as individuals. Any individual x is said to satisfy the predicate if the expression $b + d \cdot x > 0$ is true. In code:

```
newMeasure = do
    b ← sampleGaussian 0 1
    d ← newNormedVector
    return (λx → b + d · x)
newPred = do
    m ← newMeasure
    return (λx → m x > 0)
```

In addition to sampling random predicates and individuals, and evaluating expressions, we can make assumptions about them. We do this using the `observe` primitive of Borgström et al. (2013). The name of this primitive suggests that the agent observes a situation where a given proposition holds. In terms of MCMC sampling, if the argument to an *observe* call is false, then the previously sampled parameters are discarded, and a fresh run of the program is performed. In fact, in the WebPPL implementation that we use, only a portion of the sampling history may be discarded (see (Goodman and Stuhlmüller 2014) for details.) A trivial model using *observe* is the following, where one evaluates the probability of an observed fact:

```
modelSimple = do
    p ← newPred
    x ← newInd
    observe (p x)
    return (p x)
```

Even when using our approximating implementation, evaluating the above model yields certainty.

```
true : 1
```

2.2 Comparatives

We support scalar predicates and comparatives. The expression $b + d \cdot x$ can be interpreted as a degree to which the individual x satisfies the property characterised by (b, d). Thus satisfying a scalar predicate is defined as follows:

$$is :: Measure \to Pred$$
$$is\ m\ x = m\ x > 0$$

And comparatives can be defined by comparing such measures:

$$more :: Measure \to Ind \to Ind \to Prop$$
$$more\ m\ x\ y = m\ x > m\ y$$

Using these concepts we can define models like the following:

```
modelTall :: P Scalar
modelTall = do
  tall ← newMeasure
  john ← newInd
  mary ← newInd
  observe (more tall john mary)
  return (is tall john)
```

That is, if we observe that "John is taller than Mary", we will infer that "John is tall" is slightly more probable than "John is not tall".

The exact probability values that the model produces will be influenced by the priors that we apply (such as the standard deviation of Gaussian distributions), in addition to the observations that we record. Further, MCMC sampling is an approximation method, thus the results will vary from run to run. In the rest of the paper we will show results obtained from a typical run. For the above example, we get:

```
true : 0.552    false : 0.448
```

2.3 Vague predicates

We support vague predication, by adding an uncertainty to each measure we make for the predicate in question. This is implemented through a Gaussian error with a given std. dev. σ for each measure.

```
vague σ m x = m x + gaussian 0 σ
modelTall :: P Prop
modelTall = do
  tall ← vague 3 <$> newMeasure
  john ← newInd
  mary ← newInd
  hyp (more tall john mary)
  return (is tall john)
```

In this situation the tallness of John is more uncertain than before:

```
false : 0.512 true : 0.488
```

Additionally, a vague predicate allows apparently contradictory statements to hold, although with low probability, giving a fuzzy quality to the system. For example:

```
modelTallContr :: P Prop
modelTallContr = do
  tall ← vague 3 <$> newMeasure
```

$$john \leftarrow newInd$$
$$mary \leftarrow newInd$$
$$return \ (more \ tall \ john \ mary \ \wedge \ more \ tall \ mary \ john)$$

```
false : 0.77 true : 0.23
```

2.4 Generalised Universal Quantifiers

We now turn to generalised quantifiers. We need to interpret sentences such as "most birds fly" compositionally. On a standard reading, "most" can be seen as a constraint on a ratio between the cardinality of sets.

$$most(cn, vp) = \frac{\#\{x : cn(x) \wedge vp(x)\}}{\#\{x : cn(x)\}} > \theta. \tag{1}$$

for a suitable threshold θ. Translated into a probabilistic framework, we posit that the expected value of $vp(x)$ given that $cn(x)$ holds should be greater than θ.

$$most(cn, vp) = E(\mathbf{1}(vp(x)) \mid cn(x)) > \theta \tag{2}$$

where $\mathbf{1}$ is an indicator function, such that $\mathbf{1}(true) = 1$ and $\mathbf{1}(false) = 0$. In general, cn and vp may depend on probabilistic variables, and thus the above equation is *itself* probabilistic.

While taking the expected value is *not* an operation found in the language presented by Borgström et al. (2013), it is not difficult to extend their framework in this direction, because the expected value can be given a definite symbolic form:

$$most(cn, vp) = \frac{\int_{Ind} f_{\mathcal{N}}(x)\mathbf{1}(cn(x) \wedge vp(x))dx}{\int_{Ind} f_{\mathcal{N}}(x)\mathbf{1}(cn(x))dx} > \theta \tag{3}$$

where $f_{\mathcal{N}}$ denotes the density of the multivariate gaussian distribution for individuals. Further, the above can be implemented in many probabilistic programming languages, including WebPPL. In Haskell code, we write:

$$most :: Quant$$
$$most \ cn \ vp = expectedIndicator \ p > \theta$$
$$\textbf{where} \ p = \textbf{do} \ x \leftarrow newInd$$
$$observe \ (cn \ x)$$
$$return \ (vp \ x)$$

That is, we create a probabilistic program p, which samples over all individuals x which satisfy cn, and we evaluate $vp(x)$. The compound statement is satisfied if the expected value of the program p, itself evaluated using an inner MCMC sampling procedure, is larger than θ. In our examples, we let $\theta = 0.7$. Other generalised quantifiers can be defined in the same way with a different value for θ — in our examples we define *many* with $\theta = 0.6$.[3]

On this basis, we make inferences of the following kind. "If many chairs have four legs, then it is likely that any given chair has four legs". We model this sentence as follows:

$$chairExample1 = \textbf{do}$$
$$chair \leftarrow newPred$$
$$fourlegs \leftarrow newPred$$
$$observe \ (many \ chair \ fourlegs)$$
$$x \leftarrow newIndSuch \ [chair]$$
$$return \ (fourlegs \ x)$$

---

[3]It is possible, in fact desirable, to let θ be sampled (say from a beta distribution) so that its posterior would depend on linguistic and contextual inputs.

                    true : 0.821   false : 0.179

The model samples all possible parameter values (vectors/biases) for chairs and four-legged objects. Then, it discards all parameters such that $E(\mathbf{1}(four-legged(y)) \mid chair(y)) \leq \theta$ for a random individual y. In the implementation this expected value is approximated by first doing an independent sampling of a number of individuals y such that $chair(y)$ holds, and then checking the value of $four-legged(y)$ for this sample.

The evaluation of the last two statements, corresponding to $E(four-legged(x)) \mid chair(x)$, is done using another sampling of individuals, but retaining the values for chair and four-legged parameters identified in the previous sampling.

Interestingly, because the models that we are building implement generalized quantifiers through correlation of predicates, we get 'inverse' correlation as well. Therefore, assuming that "many chairs have four legs", and in the absence of further information, and given an individual x with four legs, we will predict a high probability for $chair(x)$.

$$chairExample2 :: P\ Prop$$
$$chairExample2 = \mathbf{do}$$
$$\quad chair \leftarrow newPred$$
$$\quad fourlegs \leftarrow newPred$$
$$\quad observe\ (many\ chair\ fourlegs)$$
$$\quad x \leftarrow newIndSuch\ [fourlegs]$$
$$\quad return\ (chair\ x)$$

                    true : 0.653   false : 0.347

The model's assumptions can be augmented with the hypothesis that most individuals are not chairs. This will lower the probability of being a chair appropriately.

$$chairExample3 :: P\ Prop$$
$$chairExample3 = \mathbf{do}$$
$$\quad chair \leftarrow newPred$$
$$\quad fourlegs \leftarrow newPred$$
$$\quad observe\ (many\ chair\ fourlegs)$$
$$\quad observe\ (most\ anything\ (not' \circ chair))$$
$$\quad x \leftarrow newIndSuch\ [fourlegs]$$
$$\quad return\ (chair\ x)$$

                    false : 0.779   true : 0.221

We conclude this section with a more complex example inference involving three predicates and four propositions. Assume that

1. Most animals do not fly.

2. Most birds fly.

3. Every bird is an animal.

Can we conclude that "most animals are not birds"? We model the example as follows:

$$birdExample = \mathbf{do}$$
$$\quad animal \leftarrow newPred$$
$$\quad bird \leftarrow newPred$$
$$\quad fly \leftarrow newPred$$
$$\quad observe\ (most\ animal\ (not' \circ fly))$$
$$\quad observe\ (most\ bird\ fly)$$

$$observe\ (every\ bird\ animal)$$
$$return\ (most\ animal\ (not' \circ bird))$$

And it concludes with overwhelming probability:

```
true : 0.941    false : 0.059
```

This result can be explained by the fact that only models similar to the one pictured in Figure 1 conform to the assumptions. One way to satisfy "every bird is an animal" is to assume that "animal" holds for every individual, because this is compatible with all hypotheses. Then "most animals don't fly" implies that the "fly" predicate has a large (negative) bias. Finally, "most birds fly" can be satisfied only if "fly" is highly correlated with "bird" (the predicate vectors have similar angles), *and if the bias of "bird" is even more negative than that of "fly"*. Consequently, "bird" also has a large negative bias, and the conclusion holds.

3 Semantic Learning

Bayesian models can adapt to new observations, giving rise to learning. We have seen that our framework takes account of data provided in the form of qualitative statements, including those made with generalised quantifiers. We can also accommodate information in a sequence of observed situations.

Consider the following data (which we have taken from `https://en.wikipedia.org/wiki/Naive_Bayes_classifier`).

Person	height (feet)	weight (lbs)	foot size(inches)
male	6	180	12
male	5.92	190	11
male	5.58	170	12
male	5.92	165	10
female	5	100	6
female	5.5	150	8
female	5.42	130	7
female	5.75	150	9

We feed the person and weight data into our system to see if it can learn a correlation between these two random variables.

$$model :: P\ Prop$$
$$model = \mathbf{do}$$
$$weight \leftarrow newMeasure$$

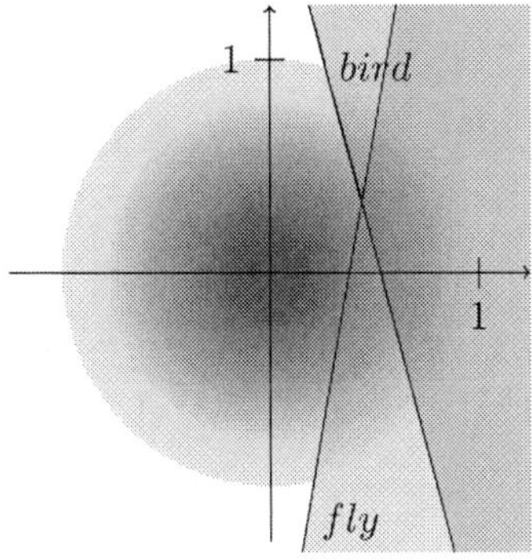

Figure 1: A probable configuration for the predicates in the bird example. (We ignore the "animal" predicate, which can be assumed to hold for every individual.) The grey area suggests the density of arbitrary individuals, a 2-dimensional Gaussian distribution in this case. Birds lie in the blue and purple areas. Flying individuals are in the red and purple shaded areas. Note that the density of individuals in the blue area is small compared to that in the purple area. In this model, the predicates "most individuals are not birds", "most individuals don't fly" and "Most birds fly" hold together.

$isMale \leftarrow newPred$

let $sampleWith :: Bool \rightarrow Float \rightarrow P\ Ind$
   $sampleWith\ male\ w = $ **do**
     $s \leftarrow newInd$
     $observe\ (isMale\ s\ `iff`\ constant\ male)$
     $observeEqual\ (weight\ s)\ (constant\ w)$
     $return\ s$

$\_ \leftarrow sampleWith\ True\ 1.80$
$\_ \leftarrow sampleWith\ True\ 1.90$
$\_ \leftarrow sampleWith\ True\ 1.70$
$\_ \leftarrow sampleWith\ True\ 1.65$
$\_ \leftarrow sampleWith\ False\ 1.00$
$\_ \leftarrow sampleWith\ False\ 1.50$
$\_ \leftarrow sampleWith\ False\ 1.30$
$\_ \leftarrow sampleWith\ False\ 1.50$

$x \leftarrow newInd$

$observeEqual\ (weight\ x)\ 1.9$
$return\ (isMale\ x)$

The data is provided as a series of observations. The Boolean observations use the usual *observe* primitive. To handle continuous data, we must add a new primitive in our implementation. In principle we could add a hard constraint on the measure of any scalar predicate, and the posterior would simply select points which satisfy exactly this constraint. However, because we are using MCMC sampling, this strategy would discard all samples that do not satisfy the constraint *exactly*. But because precise satisfaction of a constraint is stochastically impossible, all samples would be discarded and we would never obtain an approximation for the posteriors.

To avoid this problem we retain samples which do not satisfy the equality exactly, but with a specified probability, given by the expression e^{-d^2}, where d is the distance between the predicted and observed values.

With this implementation our model predicts that an individual of weight 1.9 is male with the following probabilities.

```
true : 0.57805     false : 0.42195
```

A more direct way to identify the learned correlation between weight and maleness is by measuring the cosine of the angle between the weight and male vectors. The posterior adheres to the following distribution, which indicates a strong correlation.

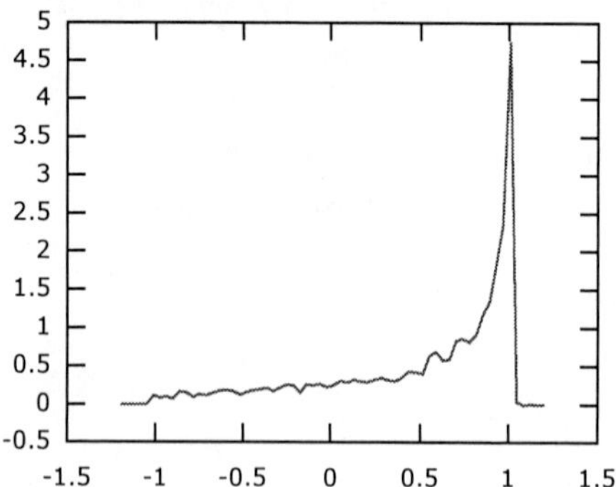

4   Related Work

van Eijck and Lappin (2012) propose a theory in which probability is distributed over the set of possible worlds. The probability of a sentence is the sum of the probability values of the worlds in which it is true. This proposal is not implemented, and it is unclear how the worlds to which probability is assigned can be represented in a computationally tractable way.[4] Van Eijck and Lappin also suggest an account of semantic learning. It seems to require the wholistic acquisition of all the classifier predicates in a language in a correlated way.

Our system avoids these problems. Our models sample only the individuals and properties (vector dimensions) required to estimate the probability of a given set of statements. Learning is achieved for restricted sets of predicates with these models.

Cooper et al. (2014) and Cooper et al. (2015) develop a compositional semantics within a probabilistic type theory (ProbTTR). On their approach the probability of a sentence is a judgment on the likelihood that a given situation is of a particular type, specified in terms of ProbTTR. They also sketch a Bayesian treatment of semantic learning.

Cooper et al.'s semantics is not implemented, and so it is not entirely clear how probabilities for sentences are computed in their system. They do not offer an explicit treatment of vagueness or probabilistic inference. It is also not obvious that their type theory is relevant to a viable compositional probabilistic semantics.

Sutton (2017) uses a Bayesian view of probability to support a resolution of classical philosophical problems of vagueness in degree predication. His treatment of these problems is insightful, and it seems to be generally compatible with our implemented semantics. But it operates at a philosophical level of abstraction, and so a clear comparison is not possible.

Goodman and Lassiter (2015) and Lassiter and Goodman (2017) construct a probabilistic semantics implemented in WebPPL. They construe the probability of a declarative sentence as the most highly valued interpretation that a hearer assigns to the utterance of a speaker in a specified context. The Goodman–Lassiter account requires the specification of considerable amounts of real world knowledge and lexical information in order to support pragmatic inference. It appears to require the existence of a univocal, non-vague speaker's meaning that hearers seek to identify by distributing probability among alternative readings. Goodman and Lassiter posit a boundary cut off point parameter for graded modifiers, where the value of this parameter is determined in context. They adopt a classical Montagovian treatment of generalised quantifiers. They also do not offer a theory of semantic learning.

By contrast we take the probability value of a sentence as the likelihood that a competent speaker would endorse an assertion given certain assumptions (hypotheses). Therefore, predication remains intrinsically vague. We do not assume the existence of a sharply delimited non-probabilistic reading for a predication that hearers attempt to converge on through estimating the probability of alternative readings. All predication consists in applying a classifier to new instances on the basis of supervised training. We do not posit a contextually dependent cut off boundary for graded predicates, but we suggest an integrated approach to graded and non-graded predication on which both types of property term allow for vague borders. Further advantages of our account include a probabilistic treatment of generalised quantifiers, which includes higher-order quantifiers like *most*, and a basic theory of semantic learning that is a straightforward extension of our sampling procedures for computing the marginal probability of a sentence in a model.

5   Conclusions and Future Work

We have presented a compositional Bayesian semantics for natural language, implemented in the functional programming language WebPPL. We represent objects and properties as vectors in n-dimensional vector spaces. Our system computes the marginal probability of a declarative sentence through MCMC sampling in Bayesian models constrained by specified hypotheses.

Our semantic framework provides straightforward treatments of vagueness in predication, gradable predicates, comparatives, generalised quantifiers, and probabilistic inferences across several property dimensions with generalised quantifiers. It avoids some of the limitations of other current probabilistic semantic theories.

---

[4]See (Lappin 2015) for a discussion of the complexity problems posed by the representation of complete worlds.

In future work we will extend the syntactic and semantic coverage of our framework. We will improve our modelling and sampling mechanisms to accommodate large scale applications more efficiently and robustly. Finally, we will develop our Bayesian learning theory to handle more complex cases of classifier acquisition.

Acknowledgements

The research reported in this paper was supported by grant 2014-39 from the Swedish Research Council, which funds the Centre for Linguistic Theory and Studies in Probability (CLASP) in the Department of Philosophy, Linguistics, and Theory of Science at the University of Gothenburg. We are grateful to our colleagues in CLASP for helpful discussion of many of the ideas presented here.

References

Barwise, J. and R. Cooper (1981). "Generalised Quantifiers and Natural Language". In: *Linguistics and Philosophy* 4, pp. 159–219.

Borgström, Johannes et al. (2013). "Measure Transformer Semantics for Bayesian Machine Learning". In: *Logical Methods in Computer Science* 9, pp. 1–39.

Clark, A. and S. Lappin (2011). *Linguistic Nativism and the Poverty of the Stimulus*. Chichester, West Sussex, and Malden, MA: Wiley-Blackwell.

Cooper, R. et al. (2014). "A Probabilistic Rich Type Theory for Semantic Interpretation". In: *Proceedings of the EACL 2014 Workshop on Type Theory and Natural Language Semantics (TTNLS)*. Gothenburg, Sweden: Association of Computational Linguistics, pp. 72–79.

– (2015). "Probabilistic Type Theory and Natural Language Semantics". In: *Linguistic Issues in Language Technology* 10, pp. 1–43.

Dowty, D. R., R. E. Wall, and S. Peters (1981). *Introduction to Montague Semantics*. Dordrecht: D. Reidel.

Goodman, N. and D. Lassiter (2015). "Probabilistic Semantics and Pragmatics: Uncertainty in Language and Thought". In: *The Handbook of Contemporary Semantic Theory, Second Edition*. Ed. by S. Lappin and C. Fox. Malden, Oxford: Wiley-Blackwell, pp. 143–167.

Goodman, N. et al. (2008). "Church: a Language for Generative Models". In: *Proceedings of the 24th Conference Uncertainty in Artificial Intelligence (UAI)*, pp. 220–229.

Goodman, Noah D and Andreas Stuhlmüller (2014). *The Design and Implementation of Probabilistic Programming Languages*. http://dippl.org. Accessed: 2018-4-17.

Lappin, Shalom (2015). "Curry Typing, Polymorphism, and Fine-Grained Intensionality". In: *The Handbook of Contemporary Semantic Theory, Second Edition*. Ed. by Shalom Lappin and Chris Fox. Malden, MA and Oxford: Wiley-Blackwell, pp. 408–428.

Lassiter, D. (2015). "Adjectival modification and gradation". In: *The Handbook of Contemporary Semantic Theory, Second Edition*. Ed. by S. Lappin and C. Fox. Malden, Oxford: Wiley-Blackwell, pp. 655–686.

Lassiter, Daniel and Noah Goodman (2017). "Adjectival Vagueness in a Bayesian Model of Interpretation". In: *Synthese* 194, pp. 3801–3836.

Montague, Richard (1974). "The Proper Treatment of Quantification in Ordinary English". In: *Formal Philosophy*. Ed. by Richmond Thomason. New Haven: Yale UP.

Sutton, Peter R. (2017). "Probabilistic Approaches to Vagueness and Semantic Competency". In: *Erkenntnis*.

van Eijck, J. and S. Lappin (2012). "Probabilistic Semantics for Natural Language". In: *Logic and Interactive Rationality (LIRA), Volume 2*. Ed. by Z. Christoff et al. University of Amsterdam: ILLC.

Detecting Linguistic Traces of Depression in Topic-Restricted Text: Attending to Self-Stigmatized Depression with NLP

JT Wolohan
Department of Information and Library Science
Indiana University - Bloomington
jwolohan@indiana.edu

Misato Hiraga
Department of Linguistics
Indiana University - Bloomington
mhiraga@indiana.edu

Atreyee Mukherjee
Department of Computer Science
Indiana University - Bloomington
atremukh@indiana.edu

Zeeshan Ali Sayyed
Department of Computer Science
Indiana University - Bloomington
zasayyed@indiana.edu

Abstract

Natural language processing researchers have proven the ability of machine learning approaches to detect depression-related cues from language; however, to date, these efforts have primarily assumed it was acceptable to leave depression-related texts in the data. Our concerns with this are twofold: first, that the models may be overfitting on depression-related signals, which may not be present in all depressed users (only those who talk about depression on social media); and second, that these models would under-perform for users who are sensitive to the public stigma of depression. This study demonstrates the validity to those concerns. We construct a novel corpus of texts from 12,106 Reddit users and perform lexical and predictive analyses under two conditions: one where all text produced by the users is included and one where the depression-related posts are withheld. We find significant differences in the language used by depressed users under the two conditions as well as a difference in the ability of machine learning algorithms to correctly detect depression. However, despite the lexical differences and reduced classification performance–each of which suggests that users may be able to fool algorithms by avoiding direct discussion of depression–a still respectable overall performance suggests lexical models are reasonably robust and well suited for a role in a diagnostic or monitoring capacity.

1 Introduction

Major depressive disorder is a serious illness that afflicts more than 1-in-15 Americans and more than 1-in-10 American young adults[1]. Depression is also the number one cause of suicide–the second leading cause of death among adolescents–and a difficult disease to treat, because those suffering from it are often reluctant to report. In part, this is true because depression is a highly stigmatized disease. Not only is stigma a significant contributor to the suffering of both clinically and subclinically depressed individuals, depression stigma is associated with lower rates of help seeking and higher rates of avoidance (Manos et al., 2009). This results in a population that may be motivated to hide or otherwise disguise their depression symptoms.

This paper examines whether a machine learning approach based on linguistic features can be used to detect depression in Reddit users when they are not talking about depression, as would be the case with those wary of depression stigma. We split this effort across two datasets: the first, we allow all the Reddit posts from a sample of 12,106 users, about half of whom are depressed, and in the second, we allow only those posts which were not directly discussing depression. With this second dataset, we intend to approximate the activity of users reluctant to discuss depression online or attempting to hide their depression.

[1] https://www.nimh.nih.gov/health/statistics/major-depression.shtml

Proceedings of the First International Workshop on Language Cognition and Computational Models, pages 11–21
Santa Fe, New Mexico, United States, August 20, 2018.
https://doi.org/10.18653/v1/P17

On each dataset we perform two sets of analysis: a lexical analysis–using LIWC (Pennebaker et al., 2015) and Term-Frequency/Inverse-Document Frequency (TF-IDF) weights–and a classification task–using a number of Support Vector Machine classifiers trained on lexical features. The first analysis reveals differences between the text produced by depressed users when the corpus is allowed to include depression-related text and when depression-related text is withheld. The second analysis reveals that the classification task is more difficult when depression-related text is withheld; however, machine learning classifiers are still able to detect linguistic traces of depression.

Our contributions with this paper are threefold. First we demonstrate the impact and potential importance of removing mental-health topics from a corpus before training natural language processing models; second, we provide attention to the task of detecting stigmatized or otherwise "hidden" depression, which has to date not been looked at by the research community; and third, we find that the linguistic patterns of depressed Reddit users are consistent with popular depression batteries and interventions.

2 Related Work

2.1 Depression detection

Language often reflects how people think, and it has been used in assessing mental health conditions by psychiatrists (Fine, 2006). Recently, computational methods have begun to be employed to study depressed users' writings and activities on social media. A meta-analysis by Guntuku et al. (2017) summarizes several iterations of the depression detection task, including clinical depression detection (De Choudhury et al., 2013b; Schwartz et al., 2014; Tsugawa et al., 2015; Preoţiuc-Pietro et al., 2015), post-partum depression prediction (De Choudhury et al., 2013a), post-traumatic stress disorder detection (Harman and Dredze, 2014; Preoţiuc-Pietro et al., 2015), and suicidal attempt detection (Coppersmith et al., 2016). For our purposes, it is most important to note how different authors operationalize the depression detection task and what assumptions are included in that approach.

The first such approach, by Coppersmith et al. (2014) (also used by Coppersmith et al. (2015) and Resnik et al. (2015)) , attempts to select a population of users with major depressive disorder by crawling for users' disclosure of diagnosis. The researchers first scrape a large, broadly relevant assortment of Tweets, before downselecting to only those Tweets which match the regular expression "I was diagnosed with [depression]". Tweets by the users identified in this way are then scraped to create a gold standard, and a control group of users can be randomly sampled and scraped from the general population.

A second, crowd-sourced-survey approach has also been used effectively (De Choudhury et al., 2013b; Tsugawa et al., 2015). In this approach, the researchers have micro-task workers (e.g., Turkers from Mechanical Turk) take two depression inventories (historically, CES-D (Radloff, 1977) and BDI (Beck et al., 1996)) and provide their social media handle. If the inventory results correlate (both indicating depression or no depression), the authors will scrape the users' social media data and place them in the depressed group or the control group.

A third, less frequently used, approach is based on community membership or participation. In this approach, users are classified as having a mood disorder–both depression (De Choudhury and De, 2014) and anxiety (Shen and Rudzicz, 2017) have been studied–when they post in a given community (typically a subreddit, as this approach has mostly been used with Reddit-data). This approach has tended more towards descriptive research and past analysis have focused exclusively on content from the identified communities.

Across all three methods, we find a shortcoming: authors largely make no effort to limit the topic of discussion. Given that the gold standards created by the first and third sampling strategies above are constructed by looking for disclosure of diagnosis or at least self-diagnosis, we can assume that these users have a higher probability of discussing depression than a typical, control group user. Algorithms trained upon these samples to predict depression may be cluing in on this topic-proclivity to achieve artificially high results. Further, all three approaches, by not removing explicit discussion of depression from their training data, at the very least can be expected to under perform on an important population: the depressed who are reluctant to speak about their condition. To our knowledge, only three studies have attempted to remedy this and each of those has been computationally (as opposed to psycho-linguistically

	All Subreddits	Depression Withheld	Pct. Change
Users–Depressed	4,947	4,324	−12.6%
Users–Control	7,159	7,153	−0.1%
Users–Total	12,106	11,477	−5.2%
Words–Depressed	55,980,678	48,399,823	−13.5%
Words–Control	93,109,041	92,787,403	−0.3%
Words–Total	149,089,719	141,187,226	−5.3%

Table 1: Dataset Composition by Tasks

oriented) oriented (Yates et al., 2017) or exploratory in nature (Losada and Crestani, 2016; Hiraga, 2017).

2.2 Depression Stigma

One of the reasons we are concerned with previous authors not removing depression-related text from their data is because we are concerned about stigma leading many depressed users to be silent about their depression. Latalova et al. (2014) suggest that stigma-related effects are an important factor preventing depression-related help-seeking among men and that a complex relationship exists between masculinity and depression. Through a narrative review of the research on stigma, they find that masculinity is both a cause of depression and a cause of reduced-help seeking, exemplified by gender norms like "boys don't cry".

Similarly, after having conducted a survey of a random sample (n=5,500+) of college students from 13 American Universities, Eisenberg et al. (2009) suggest that social-norms are a leading cause of perceived public stigma and, in turn, personal stigma. They found that higher self-stigma is associated with lower reported comfort seeking help and that self-stigma was highest among male students, Asian students, young students, poor students and religious students.

In a random sample (n=1,300+) people from the general Australian public, Barney et al. (2006) find this same pattern: higher reported self-stigma scores result in increased hesitation about seeking help for depression. Major sources of this hesitation included personal embarrassment at having depression and the perception that others would respond negatively. This last finding is in contrast to Schomerus et al. (2006), who find that among a sample (n=2,300+) of the German public anticipation of discrimination by others did not prevent help seeking behavior (though again, self-stigma was negatively associated with help seeking).

Our view is that given the consistent findings that self-stigma reduces help-seeking, depression detection efforts using social media and natural language processing have a unique opportunity to reach these individuals. If models can be trained to identify not just the depressed and open about it, but the depressed and hesitant, help could be directed to individuals who would otherwise neglect to seek it. In this study, our aim is to approximate the scenario where the users are hesitant to post about depression.

3 Method

3.1 Data

The data for this analysis are the reddit posts of 12,106 reddit users, totalling 149,089,719 words. The users are divided into two categories: depressed and not-depressed. Of the more than 12,000 users, 4,947 ($\approx 40\%$) are considered depressed and these users account for nearly 56-million words ($\approx 38\%$). The 7,159 ($\approx 60\%$) non-depressed users are responsible for the other 93-million words ($\approx 62\%$).

To gather our depressed users, we used a community participation approach similar to that employed in other Reddit-based research (De Choudhury and De, 2014; Shen and Rudzicz, 2017). We considered a user depressed if they started a thread in Reddit's depression subreddit[2]–which identifies itself as a "a supportive space for anyone struggling with depression."–as a user self-identifying as suffering from depression. On the basis of this heuristic, we scraped the 10,000 most recent post-authors from the

---

[2]www.reddit.com/r/depression

Depressed		Control	
r/depression_help	r/aww	r/AskReddit	r/news
r/AskReddit	r/Showerthoughts	r/pics	r/gaming
r/depression	r/gaming	r/funny	r/aww
r/pics	r/videos	r/Showerthoughts	r/todayilearned
r/funny	r/todayilearned	r/mildlyinteresting	r/gifs

Table 2: Some of the common subreddits the users participated in

depression subreddit. To construct a control group, we scraped users who had started a thread in Reddit's AskReddit subreddit[3], one of the site's most popular communities with more than 18 million subscribers. We believe AskReddit is a fitting control for the depression community because its question-and-answer format is similar to the information and support seeking of the Depression community, and AskReddit is among the most popular subreddits among depressed users in our sample.

With these two lists of users, we then scraped the entire available post-history of these users. Users from whom we did not collect more than 1,000 words of text were removed from our dataset. By scraping the entirety of our users posts we achieve a diverse range of conversation topics (see Table 3.1), including computer games and internet culture, politics and current events, and more. Most of the discussion sampled ($\approx 96\%$) was unrelated to depression.

Two of the authors validated our heuristic for selecting depressed Reddit users through a systematic, independent review of 150 posts from the front-page of the depression subreddit. The authors agreed on 99% (149/150) of the total classifications and both authors agreed that 147 of the 150 posts indicated at least a self-diagnosis of depression-like symptoms by the authoring user. A 99% confidence interval about this proportion suggests that no less than 92% of users selected by our depressing heuristic are suffering from self-diagnosed depression-like symptoms. We did not attempt to assess the number of depressed users in our control sample; however we would expect the upper-bound on this to be around 1-in-20[4] .

3.2 LIWC Analysis

LIWC, the Linguistic Inquiry and Wordcount Tool, is psychometric analysis software based on the idea that the words a person uses reveal information about their psychological state (Pennebaker et al., 2015). The software has been extensively used in natural language processing tasks for feature-creation, including within the area of mental-illness detection (for more, see Guntuku et al. (2017)). We use LIWC both as a source of features and as part of a stand alone analysis.

For the latter, we estimate the true means of several depression-related indices using 95% T^2 intervals (Hotelling, 1931) for the control and depressed users under our two detection conditions: (1) including all data and (2) withholding depression-related data.

3.3 Classification

With respect to classification, we endeavor to solve two tasks. The first is a benchmark designed to mirror the depression-detection efforts to date. In this task, we use all of the data from the 4,947 depressed users and 7,159 non-depressed users in our dataset. The second task is an expanded version of efforts by Hiraga (2017) which excludes the explicit discussion of depression. We achieve this by witholding posts and comments from 17 subreddits related to depression. We selected subreddits for exclusion by examining subreddits linked from the depression subreddit (e.g., r/SuicideWatch and r/mentalhealth) and snowballing out to other related subreddits. We also examined a list of subreddits frequented by depressed users for those with depression-related names. Limiting our data in this way, our dataset was reduced to only 4,324 depressed users and 7,153 non-depressed users who met our 1,000-word threshold. A comparison of these tasks is shown in Table 1.

---

[3] www.reddit.com/r/AskReddit

[4] According to the CDC, this is the rate of depression among the general public and AskReddit is a general purpose subreddit.

	All–Dep	Off–Ctrl	Off–Dep
All–Ctrl	950.1*	0.3	460.5*
All–Dep	-	1397.7*	120.4*
Off–Ctrl	-	-	475.7*
*Significant at p<.001			

Table 3: F-values of pairswise two-sample T^2 tests about the LIWC index means

For these tasks, we train two Linear Support Vector Machines (Fan et al., 2008) with TF-IDF weighted combinations of word and character $n$grams and LIWC features. Our **character** n**gram** features include all 2- to 4-grams; our **word** n**gram** features contain unigrams and bigrams; our **LIWC features** contain all the lexical indexes output by LIWC. We use a **smoothed TF-IDF** approach–implemented as $tf(t) \times \log(\frac{N+1}{n_t+1})$–where $tf(t)$ is the number of times the unigram or bigram t occurs, N is the number of documents and n_t is the number of documents containing the unigram or bigram t.

We limit our text prepossessing to sentence segmentation, tokenization, using a simple, social-media aware tokenizer[5], and ignoring case.

4 Results

4.1 LIWC Analysis

The 95% T^2 intervals about the user-level means of select depression-related indices demonstrates a wide-gap between the control users and the depressed users that narrows significantly when depression-related topics are removed from the data. We find significant differences between all group-condition differences, except for the two control groups (control users including depression text and control users with depression text withheld). Table 2 reports the F-values of all pairwise comparisons, with higher numbers indicating a greater difference between the samples.

The intervals about the specific indices reveal that depressed users are less "analytic", with less "clout" and more "authentic" than their control-group counterparts. Further, they use the personal pronoun *I* more, engage in more comparisons, speak with more affect, especially expressing more negative emotion, anxiety and sadness, with a greater emphasis on the present and future. Small to no differences are found between depressed and control users with respect to positive emotion expression (although depressed users may use more), anger, social language, family language, and focus on the past.

Between the depressed users in the all-included condition and the depressed users in the withheld condition, we find that depressed users appear more "analytic" and less "authentic" in the withheld case, with a decreased use of the *I* pronoun, decreased expression of sadness, and a decreased focus on the present. All of these changes make depressed users in the depression withheld condition more similar to control users; however, overall they are still more similar to the depressed users with all data included than to either control group.

4.2 Classification

The results from our two classification tasks in many ways reflect the differences found by the LIWC analysis. Of the four model variants–LIWC scores only, character $n$grams only, word $n$grams only, and the LIWC features plus both sets of $n$gram features–every variant achieved better performance in Task 1, which includes all the data collected, than its counterpart in Task 2. Between the four variants, the LIWC+$n$gram model achieved the best performance (81.8% accuracy in Task 1 and 78.7% accuracy in Task 2).

In the all topic case, as previously noted, we find that the LIWC+$n$gram model performs best. Its accuracy, AUC and F1-score are all better than the second best model, based on word-$n$gram features, that in turn is better than the third best model based on character-$n$gram features. The LIWC-based model performs well, achieving 78.7% accuracy.

---

[5]We use a modified version of: Christopher Potts' HappierFunTokenizing.

	Task 1: All topics		Task 2: Depression withheld	
	Control	Depression	Control	Depression
Analytic	45.67-48.22	32.79-36.16	45.75-48.30	**36.60-40.10**
Clout	52.07-54.15	43.55-47.04	52.05-54.14	44.64-48.10
Authentic	43.12-46.13	54.76-59.15	43.03-46.04	**49.65-54.15**
I	4.74-5.05	6.31-6.82	4.74-5.04	**5.79-6.29**
Comparisons	2.46-2.55	2.63-2.75	2.46-2.54	2.58-2.71
Affect	6.20-6.50	6.93-7.27	6.20-6.50	6.69-7.05
Pos. Emotions	3.80-4.06	4.05-4.32	3.80-4.06	4.01-4.31
Neg. Emotions	2.30-2.44	2.74-2.94	2.29-2.43	2.54-2.74
Anxiety	0.25-0.28	0.36-0.42	0.25-0.27	0.32-0.37
Anger	0.93-1.03	0.91-1.03	0.93-1.03	0.92-1.05
Sadness	0.37-0.40	0.60-0.68	0.37-0.40	**0.47-0.53**
Social	9.37-9.73	9.42-9.94	9.36-9.72	9.19-9.75
Family	0.34-0.39	0.30-0.36	0.34-0.39	0.29-0.36
Focus:Past	3.60-3.80	3.43-3.67	3.60-3.80	3.50-3.76
Focus:Pres.	11.50-11.82	12.96-13.43	11.49-11.81	**12.31-12.76**
Focus:Fut.	1.17-1.23	1.33-1.43	1.17-1.23	1.25-1.35

Bold text indicates a difference between treatment conditions for depressed users

Table 4: 95% T^2 interval about select LIWC results for groups across treatments

In the depression-topics withheld case, the results are similar. The composite model is the best, with word-$n$grams alone beating character-$n$grams alone and LIWC features performing the worst of all. For this second task, we also tested the best-performing model (the combined-features model) trained on the data from first task. With respect to accuracy, this model out performed all models except its counterpart combined-features model trained on the data from the second task; however, looking more holistically at the measures of performance, underwhelming AUC (73.2%) and an underwhelming F1-score (64.8%) suggest it not be quite as well calibrated as the word-$n$gram feature model.

5 Discussion

We were motivated to do this study by the concern that social media-based approaches to depression detection may be overlooking certain populations of interest, especially those who have high self-stigma. Our analysis reveals that concern to be warranted. Even within the constraints of our study design, which only approximates users who are hiding their depression symptoms, we find that there are significant differences between depressed users when they are talking about depression and depressed users when they are not.

This difference is evident looking at the F-scores presented in Table 2 and the confidence intervals in Table 4. Table 2 indicates large gaps between control and depressed users in both cases: all data permitted and depression-data witheld. Table 4 indicates the specific areas where depressed users modify their language when not discussing their depression. Overall, when not discussing depression, depressed Redditor's become more analytic and less willing to express their personal feelings, especially sadness and their present state.

We find that the depressed Redditor's language use fits within the paradigm one would expect. Beck's depress inventory (Beck et al., 1996) posits a trichotomy of depression: depressed attitude (1) towards the self, (2) towards the world, and (3) towards the future. As reflected by their LIWC scores, it is clear that depressed users more heavily emphasize themselves–seen in I usage–and the future–seen in the "Future:Focus" variable–than users who were part of our control group.

Further, these results are also consistent with a mindfulness-linked view of depression (Kabat-Zinn, 2003; Hofmann et al., 2010). Depressed users show an increase in anxious language–especially prevalent when users are talking about depression–decreased analytic language and, as previously mentioned, a

Model	Acc	AUC	F1
Task 1: All topics			
Baseline			
LIWC	.787	.751	.680
Char $n$grams	.810	.771	.707
Word $n$grams	.813	.777	.717
LIWC+$n$gram	**.818**	**.786**	**.729**
Task 2: Depression topic withheld			
Baseline			
Task 1 Best	.780	.732	.648
LIWC	.751	.706	.613
Char $n$grams	.774	.729	.646
Word $n$grams	.778	.738	.660
LIWC+$n$gram	**.787**	**.752**	**.681**

Table 5: Task 1 and Task 2 Results

strong emphasis on the self. This suggests, as the mindfulness research has (Williams, 2008; Michalak et al., 2008), that the wrong 'mode of mind', i.e., ruminating on negative thoughts, may exacerbate depressive mood.

We can further color our understanding of what depressed users are talking about by examining the words with the highest TF-IDF scores. A selection of words from the top-100 highest TF-IDF scores for depressed users is shown in Table 5. We have categorized these words into 5 groups: therapy and medication, people words, dialogic terms, Reddit and games, and porn and masturbation addiction.

Therapy and medication terms Unsurprisingly, the most common class of depression-indicator words are therapy- and medication-related terms. What is interesting, however, is the wide range of treatments about which depressed Redditors talk. They talk about talk-therapy related treatments (e.g., *psychitrist, counselor, therapist*), standard medications for depression (e.g., *Citalporam, Xanax,Prozac*, and the general: *antidepressants*), as well as alternative- or self-medications (e.g., *CBD*—THC oil, Kratom— a relatively new psychoactive). This suggests redditors are looking at a wide-range of solutions for their depression, further implying that they have been unsuccessful with previous attempts. It also suggests that Reddit may be a fruitful place to monitor the prevalence un-prescribed treatments.

People words Consistent with our LIWC analysis, in the depressed user all topic results we find personal pronouns like *I'm* and *I've*, which show users talking about themselves. This is also consistent with a notion of depressed individuals emphasizing themselves (Beck et al., 1996).

Dialogic terms Terms that are often used in conversations such as (*you, you're, yea, yeh, ur, thankyou*) show up with regularity in the top-100. This suggests that depressed users are addressing other redditors with *you* (and *youre*) more than a typical reddit user. This could be because depressed redditors engage more heavily in advice seeking and giving than standard redditors. These narration and response situations would provide ripe opportunity to address others.

Reddit, manga, games Across all user types and conditions we find Reddit-specific terms related to subreddits and gaming, such as *meirl*[6], a meme-sharing sub, *IGN*, a popular gaming website, and various game and manga characters *Nyx, warlock, Goku* and *Vegeta*.

Masturbation and pornography addiction Interestingly, a Reddit community dedicated to male sexual restraint–*nofap*–and one of its core concepts, "porn, masturbation and orgasm avoidance"–*pmo*– appear prominently in the depressed user tf-idf rankings. The stated purpose of the "NoFap" community[7] is to help users "reboot from porn addiction", by abstaining from orgasm for a month or more. This suggests that depressed Redditors, or at least a subset of them, are inclined to side with the research that has linked internet addiction, masturbation and pornography consumption with increases in depression

---

[6] www.reddit.com/r/meirl

[7] www.reddit.com/r/NoFap

Therapy and medication			People words	Dialogic terms	Reddit, games	Porn addiction
Psychiatrist	mg	Counseling	I'm	Thank you	Nyx	PMO
Xanax	Prozac	NMOM	I've	yea	IGN	nofap
Adderall	Therapist	BDP	ur	yeah	MeIRL	
Anhedonia	Counselor	ug	you			
Lucid	Zoloft	DET	you're			
Psychologist	Citalporam	Kratom	ppl			
Meds	Antidepressants	anhedonia				
ECT	CBD					

Table 6: Assorted words from top-100 most "depressed" words by TF-IDF score

(Chang et al., 2015) and depressive symptoms like loneliness (Yoder et al., 2005), as well as decreases overall health (Brody, 2010). The community appears to be mostly male users, which is perhaps not surprising; however, it is worth noting that depression has also been linked with increased rates of masturbation for women (Cyranowski et al., 2004).

Turning away from the lexical analysis to the predictive modeling, we find that the depression detection tasks mirror the LIWC findings insofar as the first task, which includes all the data, does prove to be more challenging (i.e., the models perform worse in it) than the the second task limited to depression-unrelated data. Across all the models we see a reduction in about 3% points from the all-data condition to the data-withheld condition. The one model trained on the all-data condition and tested on the data-withheld condition suffered more—about 4% points.

Relative to other depression-detection tasks, the models for the first task appear to be above average at depression detection (see Guntuku et al. (2017) for comparisons), and the performance of the LIWC-feature exclusive models suggests that the data here may be noisier than others depression-detection datasets (cf. Preoutic-Pietro et al., 2015). Given that, the 3.4% point reduction in AUC and 3.1% point reduction in accuracy should be taken seriously as a cautionary sign that depression-detection models may be overfitting for situations where social media users are open about their depression.

On a positive note, as Guntuku et al. (2017) note, these AUC scores are still better than the performance of primary-care physicians, which range from 62% to 74% (Mitchell et al., 2011). This suggests that even though social-media trained models may be overtrained, they may still be useful. Further, given that there exists a high-rate of depression-related stigma among primary care goers (Roeloffs et al., 2003), social-media based approaches may be an even more effective diagnostic tool because one can easily imagine patients with depression stigma actively acting to hide their depression from a primary care physician.

6 Conclusion

At the outset of this study, we believed that there was a chance natural language processing depression detection models were at risk of missing depressed individuals who were reluctant to talk about their depressive symptoms publicly, but nevertheless suffer substantially from depression. The results of our analysis, T^2 intervals about LIWC index scores and two classification tasks, are consistent with this belief. There appear to be substantial differences in depressed users language when they are explicitly discussing depression and when depression-related data is withheld.

With respect to the LIWC indexes, we found that depressed users showed differences with our control users as expected by psychological theory: increased anxiety, self-reference, negativity, sadness and affect, paired with decreased analytic language. With respect to the classification tasks, we found that, as expected, the depression data withheld task was more difficult than all topic task. Additionally, we found that the best performing model combined word- and character-$n$grams with LIWC features.

That said, these findings should be considered within the context of this study's limitations. First, the data shows a Reddit-specific bias (exemplified by the presence of porn/masturbation avoidance and a large number of computer, manga and video games terms in the TF-IDF rankings). These findings may not generalize to other social media platforms. Second, while depression diagnosis is temporally bounded, we make no effort to limit our data with respect to time. We may be including data for our depressed users from a time when they were not depressed, adding noise and reducing our accuracy. And third, while we intend to approximate the behavior of users who are both depressed and have high self-stigma, our attempt to do relies on users who presumably are seeking help. Users who have truly high self-stigma may behave differently. These findings and shortcomings naturally lead to future research opportunities. Future research should examine how variations in depression stigma may impact internet language use, how depressed-user language varies across social media platforms, and how language may be used to predict perceptions of public stigma. Lastly, the "NoFap" community appears like it would warrant further study on its own from a sociological perspective.

7   Ethical Considerations

This study aims to add consideration for the needs of high self-stigmatized individuals suffering from depression or depression-like symptoms. With that in mind, there are many valid reasons that people would be reluctant to disclose a mood-disorder or mental-health issue publicly. There is a difference between using computational linguistic technologies to direct targeted help towards these individuals and the use of these same technologies to expose these individuals. As long as the media continues to portray people suffering from mental illness as violent and dangerous (Friedman, 2006) and the public continues to believe that people suffering from mental illness endanger them (Barry et al., 2013), where natural language processing overlaps with health, all applications should strive to meet the classic bioethics principle of non-maleficence: first, do no harm.

Inappropriate uses of depression detection technology—especially on those with high-levels of depression stigma—may alter the way individuals relate to the disease. Individuals who feel targeted by this approach may become less likely to seek support and more likely to perceive the public as judging them for their illness. In those ways, misusing depression detection technology could exacerbate the stigma effects on a stigmatized population that is already at greater risk. Given that the goal of depression-detection for the stigmatized population is to help those individuals above all else, extra care should be paid to how the modeling is perceived by those who are suffering from depression.

References

Lisa J Barney, Kathleen M Griffiths, Anthony F Jorm, and Helen Christensen. 2006. Stigma about depression and its impact on help-seeking intentions. *Australian & New Zealand Journal of Psychiatry*, 40(1):51–54.

Colleen L Barry, Emma E McGinty, Jon S Vernick, and Daniel W Webster. 2013. After newtownpublic opinion on gun policy and mental illness. *New England journal of medicine*, 368(12):1077–1081.

Aaron T Beck, Robert A Steer, and Gregory K Brown. 1996. Beck depression inventory-ii. *San Antonio*, 78(2):490–8.

Stuart Brody. 2010. The relative health benefits of different sexual activities. *The journal of sexual medicine*, 7(4pt1):1336–1361.

Fong-Ching Chang, Chiung-Hui Chiu, Nae-Fang Miao, Ping-Hung Chen, Ching-Mei Lee, Jeng-Tung Chiang, and Ying-Chun Pan. 2015. The relationship between parental mediation and internet addiction among adolescents, and the association with cyberbullying and depression. *Comprehensive psychiatry*, 57:21–28.

Glen Coppersmith, Mark Dredze, and Craig Harman. 2014. Quantifying mental health signals in twitter. In *Proceedings of the Workshop on Computational Linguistics and Clinical Psychology: From Linguistic Signal to Clinical Reality*, pages 51–60.

Glen Coppersmith, Mark Dredze, Craig Harman, Kristy Hollingshead, and Margaret Mitchell. 2015. Clpsych 2015 shared task: Depression and ptsd on twitter. In *Proceedings of the 2nd Workshop on Computational Linguistics and Clinical Psychology: From Linguistic Signal to Clinical Reality*, pages 31–39.

Glen Coppersmith, Kim Ngo, Ryan Leary, and Anthony Wood. 2016. Exploratory analysis of social media prior to a suicide attempt. In *Proceedings of the Third Workshop on Computational Lingusitics and Clinical Psychology*, pages 106–117.

Jill M Cyranowski, Joyce Bromberger, Ada Youk, Karen Matthews, Howard M Kravitz, and Lynda H Powell. 2004. Lifetime depression history and sexual function in women at midlife. *Archives of Sexual Behavior*, 33(6):539–548.

Munmun De Choudhury and Sushovan De. 2014. s: Self-disclosure, social support, and anonymity. In *ICWSM*.

Munmun De Choudhury, Scott Counts, and Eric Horvitz. 2013a. Predicting postpartum changes in emotion and behavior via social media. In *Proceedings of the SIGCHI Conference on Human Factors in Computing Systems*, pages 3267–3276. ACM.

Munmun De Choudhury, Michael Gamon, Scott Counts, and Eric Horvitz. 2013b. Predicting depression via social media. *ICWSM*, 13:1–10.

Daniel Eisenberg, Marilyn F Downs, Ezra Golberstein, and Kara Zivin. 2009. Stigma and help seeking for mental health among college students. *Medical Care Research and Review*, 66(5):522–541.

Rong-En Fan, Kai-Wei Chang, Cho-Jui Hsieh, Xiang-Rui Wang, and Chih-Jen Lin. 2008. Liblinear: A library for large linear classification. *Journal of machine learning research*, 9(Aug):1871–1874.

Jonathan Fine. 2006. *Language in psychiatry: A handbook of clinical practice*. Equinox London.

Richard A Friedman. 2006. Violence and mental illnesshow strong is the link? *New England Journal of Medicine*, 355(20):2064–2066.

Sharath Chandra Guntuku, David B Yaden, Margaret L Kern, Lyle H Ungar, and Johannes C Eichstaedt. 2017. Detecting depression and mental illness on social media: an integrative review. *Current Opinion in Behavioral Sciences*, 18:43–49.

GACCT Harman and Mark H Dredze. 2014. Measuring post traumatic stress disorder in twitter. *In ICWSM*.

Misato Hiraga. 2017. Predicting depression for japanese blog text. In *Proceedings of ACL 2017, Student Research Workshop*, pages 107–113.

Stefan G Hofmann, Alice T Sawyer, Ashley A Witt, and Diana Oh. 2010. The effect of mindfulness-based therapy on anxiety and depression: A meta-analytic review. *Journal of consulting and clinical psychology*, 78(2):169.

Harold Hotelling. 1931. The generalization of student's ratio. *The Annals of Mathematical Statistics*, 2(3):360–378.

Jon Kabat-Zinn. 2003. Mindfulness-based interventions in context: past, present, and future. *Clinical psychology: Science and practice*, 10(2):144–156.

Klara Latalova, Dana Kamaradova, and Jan Prasko. 2014. Perspectives on perceived stigma and self-stigma in adult male patients with depression. *Neuropsychiatric disease and treatment*, 10:1399.

David E Losada and Fabio Crestani. 2016. A test collection for research on depression and language use. In *International Conference of the Cross-Language Evaluation Forum for European Languages*, pages 28–39. Springer.

Rachel C Manos, Laura C Rusch, Jonathan W Kanter, and Lisa M Clifford. 2009. Depression self-stigma as a mediator of the relationship between depression severity and avoidance. *Journal of Social and Clinical Psychology*, 28(9):1128–1143.

Johannes Michalak, Thomas Heidenreich, Petra Meibert, and Dietmar Schulte. 2008. Mindfulness predicts relapse/recurrence in major depressive disorder after mindfulness-based cognitive therapy. *The Journal of nervous and mental disease*, 196(8):630–633.

Alex J Mitchell, Sanjay Rao, and Amol Vaze. 2011. International comparison of clinicians' ability to identify depression in primary care: meta-analysis and meta-regression of predictors. *Br J Gen Pract*, 61(583):e72–e80.

James W Pennebaker, Ryan L Boyd, Kayla Jordan, and Kate Blackburn. 2015. The development and psychometric properties of liwc2015. Technical report.

Daniel Preoţiuc-Pietro, Johannes Eichstaedt, Gregory Park, Maarten Sap, Laura Smith, Victoria Tobolsky, H Andrew Schwartz, and Lyle Ungar. 2015. The role of personality, age, and gender in tweeting about mental illness. In *Proceedings of the 2nd Workshop on Computational Linguistics and Clinical Psychology: From Linguistic Signal to Clinical Reality*, pages 21–30.

Lenore Sawyer Radloff. 1977. The ces-d scale: A self-report depression scale for research in the general population. *Applied psychological measurement*, 1(3):385–401.

Philip Resnik, William Armstrong, Leonardo Claudino, Thang Nguyen, Viet-An Nguyen, and Jordan Boyd-Graber. 2015. Beyond lda: exploring supervised topic modeling for depression-related language in twitter. In *Proceedings of the 2nd Workshop on Computational Linguistics and Clinical Psychology: From Linguistic Signal to Clinical Reality*, pages 99–107.

Carol Roeloffs, Cathy Sherbourne, Jürgen Unützer, Arlene Fink, Lingqi Tang, and Kenneth B Wells. 2003. Stigma and depression among primary care patients. *General hospital psychiatry*, 25(5):311–315.

Georg Schomerus, Herbert Matschinger, and Matthias C Angermeyer. 2009. The stigma of psychiatric treatment and help-seeking intentions for depression. *European archives of psychiatry and clinical neuroscience*, 259(5):298–306.

H Andrew Schwartz, Johannes Eichstaedt, Margaret L Kern, Gregory Park, Maarten Sap, David Stillwell, Michal Kosinski, and Lyle Ungar. 2014. Towards assessing changes in degree of depression through facebook. In *Proceedings of the Workshop on Computational Linguistics and Clinical Psychology: From Linguistic Signal to Clinical Reality*, pages 118–125.

Judy Hanwen Shen and Frank Rudzicz. 2017. Detecting anxiety through reddit. In *Proceedings of the Fourth Workshop on Computational Linguistics and Clinical Psychology—From Linguistic Signal to Clinical Reality*, pages 58–65.

Sho Tsugawa, Yusuke Kikuchi, Fumio Kishino, Kosuke Nakajima, Yuichi Itoh, and Hiroyuki Ohsaki. 2015. Recognizing depression from twitter activity. In *Proceedings of the 33rd Annual ACM Conference on Human Factors in Computing Systems*, pages 3187–3196. ACM.

J Mark G Williams. 2008. Mindfulness, depression and modes of mind. *Cognitive Therapy and Research*, 32(6):721.

Andrew Yates, Arman Cohan, and Nazli Goharian. 2017. Depression and self-harm risk assessment in online forums. In *The Conference on Empirical Methods in Natural Language Processing*, pages 2968–2979.

Vincent Cyrus Yoder, Thomas B Virden III, and Kiran Amin. 2005. Internet pornography and loneliness: An association? *Sexual addiction & compulsivity*, 12(1):19–44.

An OpenNMT Model to Arabic Broken Plurals

Elsayed Issa
University of Arizona, 845 N Park Ave, Tucson, AZ 85719, USA
elsayedissa@email.arizona.edu

Abstract

The Arabic Language creates a dichotomy in its pluralization system; therefore, Arabic plurals are either sound or broken. The broken plurals create an interesting morphological phenomenon as they are inflected from their singulars following certain templates. Although broken plurals have triggered the interest of several scholars, this paper uses Neural Networks in the form of OpenNMT to detect and investigate the behavior of broken plurals. The findings show that the model is able to predict the Arabic templates with some limitations regarding the prediction of consonants. The model seems to get the basic shape of the plural, but it misses the lexical identity.

1 Introduction

The Arabic pluralization system creates an interesting phenomenon. The Arabic Language pluralizes its nouns and adjectives throughout morphologically linear as well as non-linear processes. While linear processes involve suffixation, the non-linear means involve infixation, that is, a change in the pattern of consonants and vowels inside the singular form. This phenomenon is distinguished by grammarians as broken plurals, and it is known for several Semitic languages including Arabic, Hebrew, and other Afroasiatic languages. Although several studies have examined Arabic broken plurals, this paper examines Arabic broken plurals using neural networks. The present paper attempts to build an OpenNMT neural network for training, testing and predicting broken plurals. It uses a large corpus of 2561 Arabic tokens. This attempt is twofold. It can help us approach this linguistic phenomenon using other methods, and it can explain or interpret the behavior of Arabic broken plurals templates. The importance of the present paper lies in detecting the behavior of not only broken plurals but also the behavior of sequences of consonant and vowels that make up these plurals. For instance, if the neural network can learn the singular pattern mafʕal and the plural one mafaaʕil, but it predicts the words mænðar (view) and manaaðir (views) correctly while it fails to predict markaz (center) and maraakiz (center), which both have the same patterns, then other factors are to be examined to better understand the behavior of broken plurals. Additionally, this paper addresses the L2 acquisition benefits from the technology of neural networks in predicting the behaviors of L2 learners in their acquisition of Arabic broken plurals.

The paper is organized as follows. The introduction (section 1) introduces the research questions, describes the motivation behind the paper and establishes the argument. Section 2 lays out the concrete and necessary facts about the broken plurals and their patterns. Section 3 introduces the corpus of the study. Section 4 describes the methods used such as the OpenNMT as a general-purpose and attention-based seq2seq system. Section 5 reports the general performance of the experiment. Section 6 discusses and analyses the general performance of the experiment, presents the results, and discusses the impacts of new technologies – i.e. the OpenNMT – on second language acquisition. Finally, section 7, or the conclusion briefly summarizes the results.

Proceedings of the First International Workshop on Language Cognition and Computational Models, pages 22–30
Santa Fe, New Mexico, United States, August 20, 2018.
https://doi.org/10.18653/v1/P17

2   Arabic Broken Plurals

Two types of noun and adjective plural forms are present in the morphological system of Semitic languages. They are the sound (regular) plurals and the broken (irregular) plurals. Sound plurals, on the one hand, are formed by a linear process that involves adding the suffixes -uun/-iin in case of masculine nouns/adjectives, or -aat in case of feminine nouns/adjectives.

(1) Arabic Pluralization System

	Sing.	Pl.	Gloss
(a)	*muhandis*	*muhandisuun* (nom.)/-iin (acc./gen.)	(engineer)
	ṭaliba	*ṭalibaat*	(female student)
(b)	*qalb*	*quluub*	(heart)
	mænðạr	*manaaðịr*	(view)

In (1.a), the masculine singular noun *muhandis* (engineer) is pluralized as *muhandisuun* (engineers) in the nominative case or as *muhandisiin* (engineers) as in the accusative/genitive cases. The feminine singular noun *ṭaliba* (female student) is pluralized as *ṭalibaat* (female students). On the other hand, broken plurals are formed non-linearly by means of infixation or morphological transformations that involve internal consonant and vowel changes. In (1.b), the singular noun *qalb* (heart) is pluralized as *quluub* (hearts), a plural that involves a change in the pattern of the singular from *faʕl* (CVCC) to *fuʕuul* (CVCVVC). Similarly, the singular *mænðạr (view)* is pluralized as manaaðịr, and therefore, mapped on the pattern *mafaaʕil*. Ratcliffe (1990) concludes that there are 27 broken plurals patterns applicable to Modern Standard Arabic (MSA).

Therefore, Arabic broken plurals have stimulated the interest of several scholars. The non-linear treatment of template morphology of Semitic languages dates to McCarthy (1979, 1981, 1982 ...) and much more subsequent work. Hammond's (1988) contributes to the description of root-and-template morphology through the study of Arabic broken plurals. Moreover, in their in-depth paper, McCarthy and Prince (1990) have developed their theory of Prosodic Domain Circumscription where "rules sensitive to the morphological domain may be restricted to a prosodically characterized (sub-) domain in a word or stem." In the same vein, Ratcliffe's (1990) article aims at providing a framework for the analysis of Arabic morphology that involves the relationship between concatenative and non-concatenative morphology.

As far as the computation of broken plurals is concerned, Plunkett and Nakisa (1997) provide a connectionist model to the pluralization system of Arabic. They provide an analysis of the phonological similarity structure of the Arabic Plural system. In other words, they "examine whether the distribution of Arabic nouns is suited to supporting a distributional default in a neural network, by calculating a variety of similarity metrics that identify: (1) the clustering of different classes of Arabic plurals in phonological space; (2) the relative coherence of individual plural classes; and (3) the extent to which membership in a plural class can be predicted by the nearest neighbor in phonological space" (Plunkett and Nakisa, 1997). Their analyses show that the phonological form of the singular determines its sound plural. In their model, the distribution of Arabic singulars does not support a distributional default; however, their network performed well in (1) predicting plural class using the phonological form of the singular, (2) infecting singular to plural forms, (3) and generalizing the plural class prediction task to unseen words.

3   Corpus

The data consists of 2562 tokens extracted from a large contemporary corpus, provided with morphological patterns for both the singular forms and the plural forms. The data is organized into five columns as follows: lemma ID, singular form, singular pattern, broken plural form and broken plural patterns (Attia et al., 2011). The two columns of the singular form and the broken plural form are extracted from the data, and then, they were prepared for the experiment using the R statistical language. The experiment is run for several times employing three different number of epochs; 10, 20 and 30 epochs.

4   Methods

Neural Machine Translation (NMT) has become a new evolving technology in the past few years. One of these NMTs is the OpenNMT (Open-Source Neural Machine Translation) which is a methodology for machine translation that has been "developed using pure sequence-to-sequence models" (Klein et al., 2017). This technology has become an effective approach in other NLP fields such as dialogue, parsing, and summarization. Also, Klein et al., (2017) maintain that OpenNMT was designed with three aims: (a) prioritize first training and test efficiency, (b) maintain model modularity and readability, (c) support significant research extensibility. In OpenNMT, four areas improve the effectiveness of the model. These four areas are gated RNNs such as LSTMs, large stacked RNNs, input feeding and test-time decoding (Klein et al., 2017). Although OpenNMT is built to handle sequence-to-sequence instances where it requires corpora of bilingual data to work, it can be used in other linguistic domains such as phonology and morphology.

As long as OpenNMT-py runs a neural machine translation that uses sequence-to-sequence long short-term memory (LSTM) to render a sequence of words into another sequence of words, this model uses OpenNMT as a tool that takes a sequence of broken plural letters and predicts them from a sequence of singular letters. The model deals with the non-linear morphological phenomenon of broken plurals as a machine translation problem where the input is the singular form, and the output is the plural form. The R code is used to vectorize singulars (as the input) and plurals (as the output); divide the data into one-third for validation, two-thirds for training, and 100 items for testing; and create log files for the three processes of OpenNMT; training, validation, and testing.

5   Results

Due to the small set of data, the model is run employing two stages. The first stage involves running the model for 10, 20 and 30 epochs without randomizing the data while the second stage covers the same number of epochs involving data randomization. The rationale behind this is training and testing the model for optimal results.

	Without Randomization			With Randomization		
	10 epochs	20 epochs	30 epochs	10 epochs	20 epochs	30 epochs
Prediction Average Score	-0.9190	-1.0311	-1.0610	-0.9733	-1.036	-1.0598
Validation Accuracy	55.9242	50.6183	51.4165	62.3264	62.3264	58.3398

Table (1) shows that the best results that characterize the performance of the model are at epochs 10 and 20 with a randomized data as well as 10 epochs without data randomization in case of the best prediction average score. The decline in the validation accuracy and the training accuracy can be due to: (1) the small amount of data in the corpus, (2) the small number of templates that the model learns. In addition, one assumption that validation accuracy is lower than training accuracy is the overfitting, meaning that the model learned particulars that help a better performance in the training data that cannot be applied in a large data. This, in fact, results in poor performance. Therefore, the model is run using a different number of epochs with randomization and without randomization to try to overcome the problem of overfitting.

6 Discussion and Future Work

Based on these results, several points will be addressed. First, the examination of the training data shows that the data consist of 1641 observations which are divided into three categories. These involve the broken template *ʔafʕaal* with a frequency of 384 tokens, the template *Mafaaʕil* with a frequency of 466 tokens and 791 tokens for the rest of other templates. The frequency of the measures in the training data is shown in figure (1) below. It shows that the two patterns (*ʔafʕaal* and *Mafaaʕil*) constitute more than the half of the training data; therefore, the data predicted by the model will be greatly affected by these two patterns.

Figure 1. The Frequency of Patterns in the Training Data

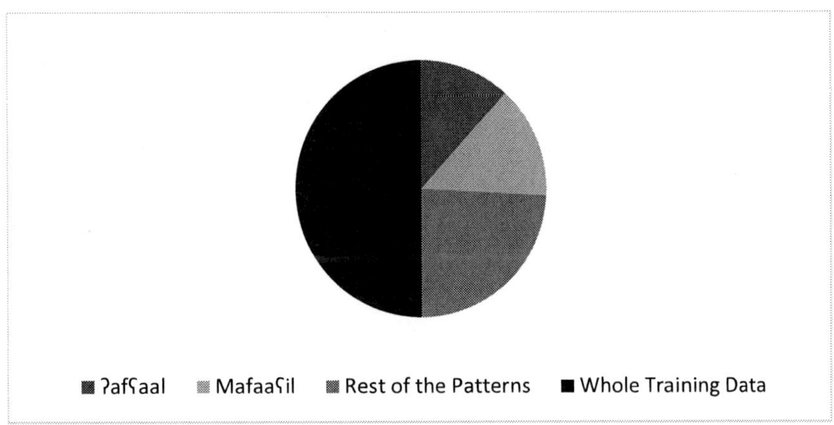

Second, the examination of the database shows that the 2562 tokens are distributed among 124 singular templates and 77 plural templates. Figure (2) below shows the most occurring patterns among the plurals ones which repeat more than 100 times. Therefore, seven templates constitute 68.73% of the database, and subsequently, they have a great effect on both processes of training and prediction. Amongst these templates are the above mentioned two templates which are found to be dominant in the training data.

Figure 2. The Frequency of Arabic Broken Plurals in the Corpus of the Study

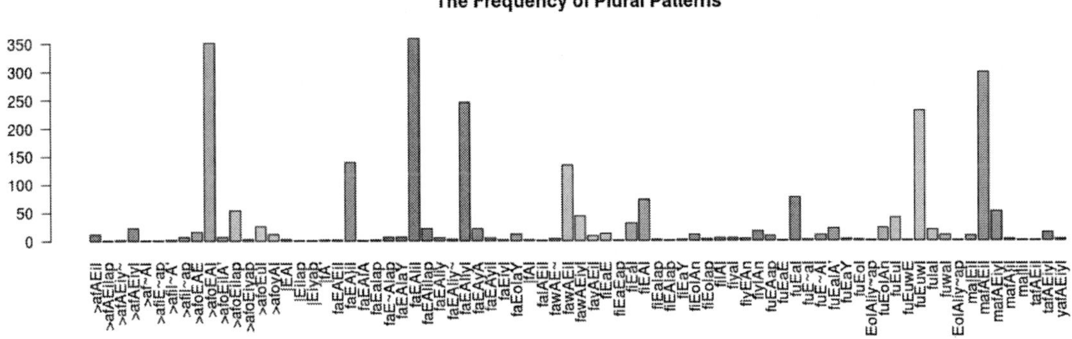

These seven frequent measures include >afoEAl (ʔafʕaal) which occurs 351 times, faEAil (Faʕaail) which occurs 140 times, faEAlil (Faʕaalil) which has 359 tokens, faEAliyl (Faʕaaliil) which occurs 259 times, fawAEil (Fawaaʕil) which has 299 tokens, fuEuwl (Fuʕuwl) with 231 frequent tokens, and mafAEiyl (Mafaaʕiil) which occurs 299 times. The predicted data demonstrate 100 predicted plurals which consist of 13 different templates. The frequency of these predicted templates is shown in figure (3) below. The most salient templates are *Ɂafʕaal* and *Ɂafaaʕl* which start with the voiceless glottal stop /Ɂ/ and *mafaaʕl* and *mafaaʕiil* which begin with the prefix /ma-/.

Figure 3. The Frequency of the Plural Templates in the Predicted Data

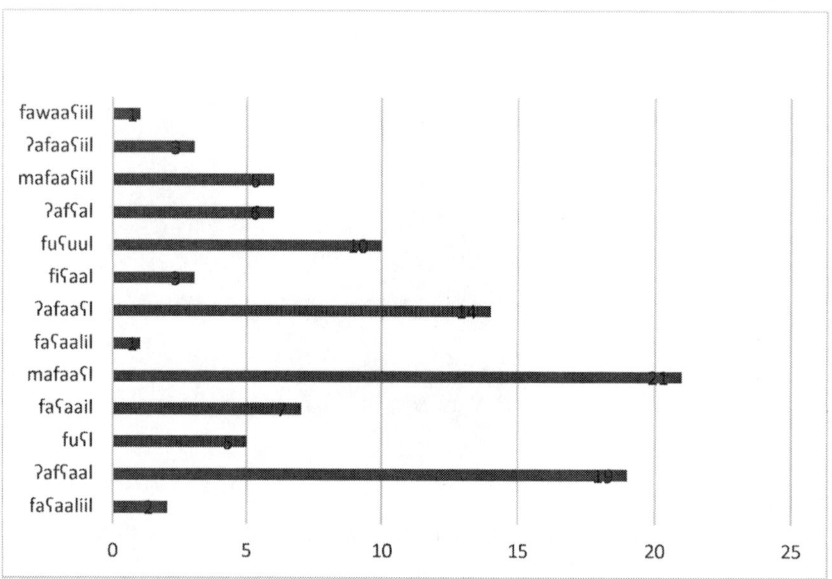

Considering this information in addition to the information introduced earlier about the frequency of *Ɂafʕaal* and *Mafaaʕil* in the training data, it can be inferred that the predicted data is highly influenced by the two prefixes Ɂa- and ma-. Accordingly, the data show that all the predicted plurals by the model involve templates that start with either the glottal stop /Ɂ/ or the prefix ma-. The prediction of the data demonstrates an interesting phenomenon. Although the number of the template *Mafaaʕil* outnumbers the *Ɂafʕaal* in the training data as illustrated in figure (1) above, the model predicts the templates with the prefix Ɂa- more than the prefix ma-. This is, in fact, due to the frequency of patterns starting with the Ɂa- prefix as illustrated in figure (3) above. Also, there are many templates, which do not belong to either Ɂa- or ma- tokens, are assigned patterns starting with these two prefixes. Another interesting phenomenon is that the model can predict the structure of the pattern correctly in more than of the 60% of the predicted data. However, the model always changes one or two consonants and keeps the vowels in their slots within the template. In other words, the overall mapping of consonants and vowels to the patterns is successfully predicted as will be shown in the following discussion.

Figure 4. The Model Predictions with the Only Ɂa- and ma- Prefixes.

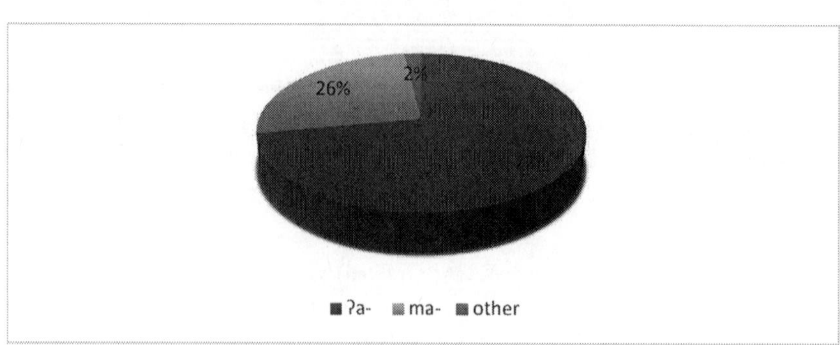

The model succeeds in predicting most of the templates meaning that it manages to predict and map the vowels on the skeleton of the template while it fails to predict the consonants. The model's prediction of consonants ranges from predicting most of them, putting restrictions on the prediction of certain consonants such as gutturals and emphatics, and assigning divergent templates. The following discussion follows by examining the most salient patterns created by the model. The pattern *ʔafʕaal* is one of the most frequent plurals in the training as well as the predicted data.

(2) The Template ʔafʕaal

	Sing.	Pl.	Predicted Pl.	Gloss
(c)	Dawor /dawr/	>adowAr /ʔadwaar/	>arowAr /ʔarwaar/	(role)
	nawo' /nawʕ/	>anowAE /ʔanwaaʕ/	>anowAn /ʔanwaan/	(type)
	ku$ok /kušk/	>ako$Ak /ʔakšaak/	>awowAn /ʔawwaan/	(kiosk)
(d)	Sawot /ṣawt/	>aSowAt /ʔaṣwaat/	>awowAn /ʔawwaan/	(voice)
	DiEof /ḍiʕf/	>aDoEAf /ʔaḍʕaaf/	>arowAn /ʔarwaan/	(double)
	HawoD /ḥawḍ/	>aHowAD /ʔaḥwaaḍ/	>awowAn /ʔawwaan/	(basin)

According to the data shown in (2) above, the model is successful in predicting the plural pattern CVC.CVVC. However, it fails to keep the same consonants while it maintains the vowels. For instance, the first broken plural in (2.c) ʔadwaar (roles) is predicted as ʔarwaar where the voiced apical trill roll /r/ replaces the voiced apico-dental stop /d/. As for the second plural in (2.c), the model alternates the final guttural fricative /ʕ/ with the voiced alveolar nasal /n/. This can be attributed to the behavior of guttural in final position as there are other examples in the data that show the unpredictability of guttural sounds in final position. In (2.d), the model is successful in predicting the pattern; albeit with more changes in the consonants. It fails to predict the emphatics /ṣ/ and /ḍ/ whether in initial or final position. This may have two interpretations; the emphatics are either non-frequent in the distribution of Arabic consonants across the Arabic roots or their behavior restricts their predictability.

(3) The Template mafaaʕil

	Sing.	Pl.	Predicted Pl.	Gloss
(e)	maSonaE /maṣnaʕ/	maSAniE /maṣaaniʕ/	manA}iy /manaaʔii/	(factory)
	mafoSil /mafṣil/	mafASil /mafaaṣil/	manA}iy /manaaʔii/	(hinge)
	manoHaY /manḥii/	manAHiy /manaaḥii/	manA}iy /manaaʔii/	(prohibited)

Although the model is successful in predicting the template structure CV.CVV.CVC and the distribution of vowels within the template, it fails to predict the consonants. In (3.e), the model predicts the prefix ma- and the vowels where it could not predict the gutturals and the emphatics. Also, the model assigns the same predicted plural to three plurals. Also, the model inserts the /}/, the hamza /ʔ/ that has a seat in the middle of the word, into this template because it resembles another template which is *faʕaaʔil* as shown below.

(4) The Template faʕaaʔil

	Sing.	Pl.	Predicted Pl.	Gloss
(f)	Ea$iyrap /ʕašiiraa/	Ea$A}ir /ʕašaaʔir/	marA}iy /maraaʔii/	(tribe)
	ZaEiynap /ðạ ʕiinaa/	ZaEA}in /ðạ ʕaaʔin/	>awA}iy /ʔawaaʔii/	(wife)
	wadiyEap /wadiiʕaa/	wadA}iE /wadaaʔiʕ/	>awA}iy /ʔawaaʔii/	(deposit)

In (4.f), the model predicts the template as CV.CVV.CVC which fits two patterns; *mafaaʕil* and *faʕaaʔil*. It also predicts the seated hamza. According to the cases in (3 and 4) above, it seems that the model learns the template, but it does not learn the distribution of the appropriate consonants on the template except for few consonants.

These observations can be attributed to examining the behavior of consonants. The frequency of certain consonants in the training data affects the model to predict specific consonants and rejects predicting the others. Therefore, there can be another experiment that examines consonants only. In other words, the experiment can involve only the consonantal tier of the broken plural. Since the Arabic morphology is interpreted in in terms of the CV-template, the study of the behavior, the frequency and the distribution of the consonants in the Arabic template can contribute to the prediction of the plural. According to the data used in this paper, it can be attested that certain consonants can occur more than other consonants in the template, i.e. the voiceless glottal stop /ʔ/. In the same manner, this proposes several questions about the distribution of some specific sounds, such as gutturals or emphatics, across the Arabic templates and the ability of neural networks, and hence, the human mind of predicting these sounds. If the predicted tokens are to be compared to plurals produced by children or L2 learners, the assumption of the difficulty of learning and predicting gutturals and emphatics will be attested. I assume that neural network is telling us about the difficulty of learning these sounds as human learners do.

(5) The Template fuʕal

Sing.	Pl.	Predicted Pl.	Gloss
(g) rasuwl /rasuul/	rusul /rusul/	>arowAr /ʔarwaar/	(prophet)
tuhomap /tuḥmaa/	tuham /tuḥam/	>awAmim /ʔawaamim/	(accusation)

These are examples of how the model fails in predicting the template. Instead, it provides the template for the pattern ʔafʕaal. There are two assumptions for this prediction. First, the big frequency of the pattern ʔafʕaal contributes to this prediction. Second, the model maps the broken plural that has the pattern *fuʕal* to the singular pattern of the pattern ʔafʕaal, and therefore, it predicts the plural as ʔafʕaal as shown in the three examples in (5.g). For example, the broken plural *rusul* (prophets) in (5.g) can be analogized to the singular *dawr* (role) – this is the singular of the pattern ʔafʕaal – in (2.c) above. Hence, the model provides the predicted pattern ʔafʕaal (CVC.CVVC) to the broken plural with the pattern *fuʕal* (CV.CVC). All the predicted plurals for the plural with the template *fuʕal* have the template ʔafʕaal in the data predicted by the model. Therefore, the future work requires examining the broken plural in a larger corpus that also includes the Arabic sound plurals.

7   L2 Acquisition and Neural Networks

The conventional methods of teaching these broken plurals to L2 learners hold that there is a template for the plural to which the learner maps the stem of the singular into different syllable patterns by shifting the consonants of the singular form. Moreover, learners are told to use their "phonographic memory" to help them learn these patterns (Brustad et al., 2011, p. 30). For instance, given the singular form *dars* (lesson) and the plural template *fuʕuul*, they are asked to provide the plural form as follows:

(6) Mapping singular form to plural template:

fuʕuul (template)
duruus (lessons)

They ignore the vowels and map the consonants to the root (f-ʕ-l) in the template; then they copy the vowels according to the melody that the template produces. The OpenNMT model is successful to some extent in capturing the melody of the template through assigning the vowels in their correct slots. However, the cases in which the model fails to capture the melody and assign the vowel, it predicts divergent plurals. Additionally, the model was successful in mapping the consonants and the vowels to the skeleton of the template as L2 learners can do and produce a correct template in approximately half of the data. The failure of the model to predict gutturals and emphatics can be attributed to two factors. First, gutturals and emphatics might have less frequency than other sounds. Second, the model is behaving like an L2 learner who is learning according to the principle of the order of acquisition; namely, learning the easiest first, then the hardest. Probably, the model is addressing one of the arguments proposed by several studies that these sounds are the hardest to learn in the Arabic language. Therefore, more work should be done to address the benefits of neural networks technology in helping the acquisition of languages by foreign learners.

8   Conclusion

This paper attempts to look at Arabic broken plurals from the perspective of neural networks by implementing an OpenNMT experiment to predict the Arabic broken plurals. Broken plurals show an interesting phenomenon in Arabic morphology as they are formed by shifting the consonants of the syllables into different syllables patterns, which in turn, changes the pattern of the word. Therefore, they produce a melody besides changing the consonants. The paper seeks to describe these plurals using another method, i.e. OpenNMT, and detecting the way these patterns behave.

The findings show that several factors contributed to the predicted plurals. These include the frequencies of some templates as well as the distribution of consonants in the training data. Accordingly, the model predicts the templates most of the time with some alternations in the consonantal tier of the template, and it sometimes gets a different plural as a prediction of another plural. However, it succeeds to learn and predict the melodic tier of the template, i.e., it predicts the distribution of the vowels within the template. This prediction of vowels is similar to the way L2 learners learn to produce the broken plural given the singular form and the plural template. Therefore, another experiment can be implemented using the consonantal tier of the template for more inspection of these plurals.

Acknowledgements

I would like to thank Professor Michael Hammond for his help, excellent instruction, and insightful comments and suggestions.

References

Attia, M., Pecina, P., Tounsi, L., Toral, A., van Genabith, J. (2011). *Lexical Profiling for Arabic. Electronic Lexicography in the 21st Century*. Bled, Slovenia. Retrieved from: https://sourceforge.net/projects/broken-plurals/

Brustad, K., Al-Batal, M., Al-Tonsi, A. (2011). *Al-Kitaab fii Ta'allum al-'Arabiyya*. Part one. 3rd edition. USA: Georgetown University Press.

Hammond, M. (1988) Templatic Transfer in Arabic Broken Plurals. *Natural Language and Linguistic Theory*. (6) 247- 270.

Hammond, M. (2018). Neural Nets for Phonology and Morphology. R codes are retrieved from https://faculty.sbs.arizona.edu/hammond/ling696b-sp18/

Klein, G., Y. Kim, Deng, Y. Y., Senellart, J. & Rush, A.M. (2017) *OpenNMT: Open-source Toolkit for Neural Machine Translation*. ArXiv e-prints1701.02810.

McCarthy, J. (1982). "A Prosodic Account of the Arabic Broken Plurals." *Current Trends in African Linguistics*, 1.25. Retrieved from https://scholarworks.umass.edu/linguist_faculty_pubs/25

McCarthy, J. & Prince A. (1990) "Prosodic Morphology and Templatic Morphology." In Mushira Eid and John McCarthy (eds.) *Perspectives on Arabic Linguistics II: Papers from the Second Symposium on Arabic Linguistics.* Amsterdam: John Benjamins. 1-54.

Plunkett, K. & Nakisa, R., C. (1997) A Connectionist Model of the Arabic Plural System. *Language and Cognitive Processes,* 12:5-6, 807-836, DOI: 10.1080/016909697386691.

Enhancing Cohesion and Coherence of Fake Text to Improve Believability for Deceiving Cyber Attackers

Prakruthi Karuna, Hemant Purohit, Özlem Uzuner, Sushil Jajodia, Rajesh Ganesan
Center for Secure Information Systems
George Mason University
{pkaruna, hpurohit, ouzuner, jajodia, rganesan}@gmu.edu

Abstract

Ever increasing ransomware attacks and thefts of intellectual property demand cybersecurity solutions to protect critical documents. One emerging solution is to place fake text documents in the repository of critical documents for deceiving and catching cyber attackers. We can generate fake text documents by obscuring the salient information in legit text documents. However, the obscuring process can result in linguistic inconsistencies, such as broken co-references and illogical flow of ideas across the sentences, which can give away the fake document and render it *unbelievable*.

In this paper, we propose a novel method to generate *believable* fake text documents by automatically improving the linguistic consistency of computer-generated fake text. Our method focuses on enhancing syntactic cohesion and semantic coherence across discourse segments. We conduct experiments with human subjects to evaluate the effect of believability improvements in distinguishing legit texts from fake texts. Results show that the probability to distinguish legit texts from believable fake texts is consistently lower than from fake texts that have not been improved in believability. This indicates the effectiveness of our method in generating believable fake text.

1 Introduction

The rise in the number of cyberattacks, such as the WannaCry ransomware attack[1], has put pressure on governments and corporations to protect their intellectual property and critical documents. Traditional cybersecurity solutions such as access-control, firewalls, malware scanners, intrusion detection and prevention technologies are limited in keeping an attacker from stealing information once he penetrates a computer network. Therefore, recent research has focused on content-based cybersecurity solutions for deceiving an attacker (Rowe and Rrushi, 2016; Jajodia et al., 2016; Heckman et al., 2015) who may succeed in gaining access to the network. These solutions generate and deploy documents with fake content (called 'honeyfiles' or 'decoy files') in the data repositories of legit documents for misleading attackers with false information. Fake documents can be either low interaction honeyfiles such as empty documents with similar names as legit documents, or high interaction honeyfiles with believable but non-informative content that can mislead the attackers (Whitham, 2017; Bowen et al., 2009). However, generating fake content that can deceive a human reader and is indistinguishable from legit content is a challenging task. This research investigates a novel linguistics approach to generate high interaction honeyfiles with believable fake text that are capable of eliciting trust.

The state of the art methods for fake text document generation (Rauti and Leppanen, 2017; Whitham, 2017) are broadly categorized based on the nature of content generated as follows: (1) random character generation, (2) generation based on random word and sentence extraction from a given public document corpus, (3) rule-based and preset template-based text generation, (4) generation based on translation from one language to another containing partial content from an existing document, and lastly, (5) generation based on language models built from a collection of similar documents (Whitham, 2017; Voris et al., 2012). However, several of the resulting automatically generated text suffers from lack of believability,

---

[1]https://www.tripwire.com/state-of-security/security-data-protection/cyber-security/10-significant-ransomware-attacks-2017/

Proceedings of the First International Workshop on Language Cognition and Computational Models, pages 31–40
Santa Fe, New Mexico, United States, August 20, 2018.
https://doi.org/10.18653/v1/P17

i.e. linguistic inconsistencies and disfluencies give it away as fake text. Believability is essential to the success of cyber deception (Voris et al., 2013). Our goal is to automatically generate believable fake documents that can deceive attackers.

The believability of a given fake text for a human reader is difficult to assess (Bowen et al., 2009; McNamara and Kintsch, 1996; Otero and Kintsch, 1992). Believability has two major factors: first, the prior knowledge of a reader (attacker) and second, the characteristics of the text. While prior knowledge can affect the believability of text, such knowledge can vary from attacker to attacker, resulting in different degrees of believability for different attackers. Textual characteristics, on the other hand, can affect believability even for attackers with no prior knowledge. We hypothesize that cohesion and coherence of text are two major factors in this respect.

We define a fake text in this research as a modified version of a legit human-written text created automatically by removing some sentences that contain salient information. We define a believable fake text as the modified version of a fake text with higher cohesion and coherence than the fake text. Prior research provides metrics for measuring cohesion and coherence based on linguistic characteristics of text (McNamara et al., 2014; Lin et al., 2011; Lapata and Barzilay, 2005). Also, the literature on text simplification and summarization provides techniques to improve cohesion and coherence of a given text (Narayan, 2014; Siddharthan et al., 2011; Mani et al., 1999). However, the question of how to effectively manipulate a given text to improve its cohesion and coherence so as to render it believable still requires more investigation.

Our specific research questions are the following: a) how can we adapt existing NLP techniques to automatically modify a given fake text to increase its cohesion and coherence? and b) what is the relation between cohesion, coherence, and believability of a given text for a reader? We study syntactic cohesion at the local sentence level and semantic coherence at the paragraph level. We evaluate our method in two ways. First, we test for a statistically significant increase in the cohesion and coherence of a believable fake text over its corresponding (unbelievable) fake text. Second, we conduct a 'believability test' (Bowen et al., 2009) with human subjects for identifying the legit text from a given pair of legit and believable fake texts. Our results show that the probability to distinguish a legit text against a believable fake text is less than 50%, while that against a (unbelievable) fake text is greater than 50%. These results indicate the effectiveness of our method in generating believable fake texts. Our specific contributions are the following:

1. A novel computational method to increase the cohesion and semantic coherence of a fake text to enhance believability.

2. An analysis of effects of this method on the human perception of text's believability.

The rest of the paper is organized as follows. Section 2 describes the related work on cohesion and coherence. Section 3 defines the required notations for our approach, which is described in Section 4. Section 5 describes our experimental setup, followed by result analysis in Section 6.

2 Related Work

We describe three most relevant areas in the literature to guide our methodology for improving the believability of a fake text.

2.1 Measuring Cohesion and Coherence of Text

McNamara et al. (2014) defines cohesion as "a characteristic of the text that can be computationally measured", whereas coherence is viewed as "the cognitive correlate of cohesion". Though cohesion and coherence measures have been used for evaluating student's essays (Burstein et al., 2010; Miltsakaki and Kukich, 2000), they are heavily used for evaluating automatically generated text summaries and the output of machine translation (Lapata and Barzilay, 2005). These measures describe the overlap of ideas in adjacent sentences or paragraphs. The publicly available systems of Coh-Metrix (McNamara et al., 2014) and the Tool for Automatic Analysis of Cohesion (TAACO) (Crossley et al., 2016) provide quantitative measures for cohesion, which are suitable to adapt in our research.

Lapata and Barzilay (2005) have proposed a quantitative measure of coherence based on the degree of connectivity across sentences using semantic similarity metrics. We adapt and extend their method to calculate coherence across paragraphs by computing semantic similarity between adjacent paragraphs.

2.2 Methods to Summarize and Simplify Text

Text summarization methods select salient sentences to form a short summary of the given text (Nenkova and McKeown, 2012; Erkan and Radev, 2004). Generated summaries are then smoothed to create a coherent whole out of these salient sentences (Siddharthan et al., 2011; Mani et al., 1999).

Our goal is different from text summarization, as we find salient sentences to remove them in order to reduce the knowledge that an attacker can comprehend from the document. Our approach then needs to create a coherent whole out of the remainder of the document when salient sentences are deleted. While both tasks (i.e., text summarization and believable fake document generation) find salient sentences, they focus on cohesion and coherence of different types of text units.

Another relevant research is to simplify text at the sentence and lexical levels for smoothing the generated text. Sentence level methods simplify the grammatical constructions with fewer number of modifiers (Narayan, 2014). Lexical level methods minimize the number of unique words occurring in the text (McNamara et al., 2014; Siddharthan, 2006). However, these methods are not designed to directly address the problem of linguistic inconsistency across the sentences.

2.3 Measuring Believability of Computer-generated Fake Text

An approach to measure believability of a fake text depends on the type of fake text. Fake texts can be categorized into three broad classes (Almeshekah and Spafford, 2016): manufacturing reality (curating false information from multiple documents), altering reality (modifying information in an existing document), and hiding reality (obscuring information in an existing document). A believable fake text lies at the intersection of altering reality and hiding reality. Prior literature has investigated different methods to compute the believability of such fake texts. Whitham et al. (2015) computed the difference between the k-dimensional linguistic features (e.g., word count, sentence length) of a fake text and legit text in a data repository. However this method does not evaluate the measure of believability for a human. Shabtai et al. (2016) and Bowen et al. (2009) conducted a realistic test where human readers were asked to identify the legit text from a pair of fake and legit texts. Similar to their work, we employ a believability test (more details in Section 6) to evaluate the automatically generated believable fake text.

3 Notations and Definitions

A legit text document d is used to generate a fake text document d', which is then used to generate a believable fake text document d''. Each of the documents d, d', and d'' consists of a sequence of sentences S that are grouped into K paragraphs (denoted by k_e). We define $s_i \in S$ as a salient sentence in d. The context of s_i is denoted by $c(s_i)$, where $c(s_i)$ consists of adjacent paragraphs containing $2x$ number of sentences with x number of sentences before and after s_i respectively. We define s_j to be a sentence in $c(s_i)$ that adjacently follows s_i. Document d is parsed to list the part of speech (POS) tags for each of the words in d and the list of POS tags is represented by POS_tag_list. Pronouns are recognized as p, noun phrases are recognized as n and a set of noun phrases are denoted by N. A noun phrase n follows a regular expression pattern of $Adjective * Noun+$.

Our technical approach aims to increase the cohesion and semantic coherence of a given fake text. To compute these two concepts, we use the measures of referential cohesion and semantic similarity based coherence.

Referential cohesion measures the overlap of ideas by measuring the linguistic overlap in the content words across adjacent paragraphs. We use the "adjacent_overlap_all_para" metric provided by TAACO (Crossley et al., 2016). This specific measure is defined as the number of overlapping lemma types that occur in both k_e and k_{e+1}. We compute the referential cohesion of a document d as follows:

$$Referential\_cohesion(d) = \frac{\sum\limits_{e=1}^{count(K)-1} Referential\_cohesion(k_e, k_{e+1})}{count(K) - 1} \qquad (1)$$

where k_e and k_{e+1} are adjacent paragraphs and $count(K)$ is the number of paragraphs in d.

Semantic coherence measures the overlap of ideas by assessing semantic similarity between the adjacent sentences or paragraphs. We adapt the measure proposed by Lapata and Barzilay (2005) to compute the coherence as follows:

$$Semantic\_coherence(d) = \frac{\sum\limits_{e=1}^{count(K)-1} sim(k_e, k_{e+1})}{count(K) - 1} \qquad (2)$$

where $sim(k_e, k_{e+1})$ is a measure of semantic similarity between adjacent paragraphs k_e and k_{e+1}.

We compute semantic similarity between two adjacent sentences or paragraphs using the semantic textual similarity system provided by UMBC-EBIQUITY-CORE (Han et al., 2013). This measure is based on the assumption that if two text sequences are semantically equivalent, we should be able to align their words or expressions. The alignment quality that serves as the similarity measure is computed by aligning similar words and penalizing poorly aligned words. Words or expressions are aligned using a word similarity model based on a combination of Latent Semantic Analysis (Deerwester et al., 1990) and semantic distance in the WordNet knowledge graph (Mihalcea et al., 2006).

4 Problem Statement and Solution Methodology

Problem Statement - Given an original legit text document d, generate a fake text document d' and a believable fake text document d'', where:

1. d' is fake by not containing a salient sentence s_i that is present in d,

2. d'' is believably fake by not containing a salient sentence s_i, and by following the constraints: $(Referential\_cohesion(d'') - Referential\_cohesion(d')) > 0$, and $(Semantic\_coherence(d'') - Semantic\_coherence(d')) > 0$.

Our proposed solution for believable fake text generation consists of two modules: A fake generation module and a believability module. The fake generation module consists of two operations: salient sentence identification and salient sentence deletion. The believability module consists of three operations: coreference correction, singleton entity removal, and referential cohesion improvement. We next describe each of these modules and link them to the specific functions provided in *algorithm 1*.

4.1 Fake generation module

Input: Legit text document d.
Output: Fake text document d' and deleted sentence s_i.
Objective: Generate fake text by deleting a salient sentence.
Salient sentence identification: This operation identifies the most salient sentence s_i in d using the LexRank algorithm (Erkan and Radev, 2004). LexRank computes sentence salience based on eigenvector centrality on the sentence similarity matrix, where sentence similarity is computed using idf-modified cosine similarity function.
Salient sentence deletion: This operation generates a fake text document d' by deleting s_i from the original document d.

Input: d', s_i, POS_tag_list, θ

Output: d''

1: **procedure** BELIEVABLE_GENERATOR(d', s_i, POS_tag_list, θ)
2:      $temp_d'' = $ COREFERENCE_CORRECTION(d', s_j, POS_tag_list)
3:      $c(s_i) = $ SINGLETON_ENTITY_REMOVAL(s_i, $c(s_i)$, θ)   ▷ $c(s_i)$ is extracted from $temp\_d''$
4:      $c(s_i) = $ REFERENTIAL_COHESION_IMPROVEMENT(s_i, $c(s_i)$, θ)
5:      $d'' = $ replace $c(s_i)$ in d' with the generated $c(s_i)$
6:      return d''
7: **end procedure**
8: **function** COREFERENCE_CORRECTION(d', s_j, POS_tag_list)
9:      **if** s_j contains p **then**   ▷ p in POS_tag_list
10:         compute coreference chains CC on d'
11:         **if** (p resolved to n in CC) & (s_j does not contain n) **then**   ▷ n in POS_tag_list
12:             replace p with n
13:         **end if**
14:     **end if**
15:     return d'
16: **end function**
17: **function** SINGLETON_ENTITY_REMOVAL(s_i, $c(s_i)$, θ)
18:     Parse N_s from s_i and $N_{c(s_i)}$ from $c(s_i)$
19:     **for** each n_1 in N_s **do**
20:         **if** (n_1 not in $c(s_i)$) or (n_1 occurs more than once in $c(s_i)$) **then**
21:             Remove n_1 from N_s
22:         **end if**
23:     **end for**
24:     **for** each n_1 in N_s **do**
25:         $n_2 = $ FIND_SEMANTICALLY_SIMILAR(n_1, $N_{c(s_i)}$, θ)   ▷ n_2 in $N_{c(s_i)}$
26:         **if** REPLACEABLE(n_1, n_2) == TRUE **then**
27:             Replace n_1 with n_2 in $c(s_i)$
28:         **end if**
29:     **end for**
30:     return $c(s_i)$
31: **end function**
32: **function** REFERENTIAL_COHESION_IMPROVEMENT(s_i, $c(s_i)$, θ)
33:     Parse N_{before} from $S \in c(s_i)$ preceding s_i and Parse N_{after} from $S \in c(s_i)$ succeeding s_i
34:     **for** each n_1 in N_{before} **do**
35:         $n_2 = $ FIND_SEMANTICALLY_SIMILAR(n_1, N_{after}, θ)   ▷ n_2 in N_{after}
36:         **if** REPLACEABLE(n_1, n_2) == TRUE **then**
37:             Replace n_1 with n_2 in $c(s_i)$
38:         **end if**
39:     **end for**
40:     return $c(s_i)$
41: **end function**

4.2 Believability module

Input: Fake text document d', deleted sentence s_i, list of POS tags POS_tag_list and semantic similarity threshold between noun phrases θ.

Output: Believable fake text document d''.

Objective: Generate believable fake text by improving cohesion and coherence of text.

Next, we describe the three key sequential operations in the believability module. These operations are performed at the word level. The parts of speech of every word in d is recognized using Stanford's CoreNLP toolkit (accuracy on noun phrase tagging = 89.30%) and saved as a list - POS_tag_list.

Coreference correction (COREFERENCE_CORRECTION(d', s_j, POS_tag_list)): The purpose of this operation is to improve the ease of reading and to relate the noun phrases in $c(s_i)$. It identifies the coreference chains in the fake text using the Stanford's CoreNLP toolkit. If a pronoun p in s_j is resolved to a noun n_2, and n_2 does not occur in s_j then replace p with n_2.

Singleton entity removal (SINGLETON_ENTITY_REMOVAL(s_i, $c(s_i)$, θ): The purpose of this operation is to hide the traces of s_i in $c(s_i)$. Specifically, if there exists a noun phrase n_1 in s_i that occurs only once in $c(s_i)$ after s_i has been deleted; then, n_1 is replaced with a semantically similar noun phrase n_2 present in $c(s_i)$ (FIND_SEMANTICALLY_SIMILAR(n_1, $N_{c(s_i)}$, θ)).

Referential cohesion improvement (REFERENTIAL_COHESION_IMPROVEMENT(s_i, $c(s_i)$), θ): The purpose of this operation is to increase the cohesive relationships between the before and after parts of s_i in $c(s_i)$. First, we extract two lists of noun phrases N_{before} and N_{after} from $c(s_i)$. N_{before} is the list of noun phrases that occur in $c(s_i)$ before s_i, whereas the N_{after} is the list of noun phrases that occur in $c(s_i)$ after s_i. Second, noun phrases in N_{before} and N_{after} are compared to pair the noun phrase n_1 in N_{before} with a semantically similar noun phrase n_2 in N_{after} (FIND_SEMANTICALLY_SIMILAR(n_1, N_{after}, θ)). Finally, n_1 is replaced with n_2 in $c(s_i)$. An example of n_1 and n_2 are "methods" and "techniques" respectively.

Both singleton entity removal and referential cohesion improvement operations replace the noun phrase n_1 with another noun phrase n_2 provided n_2 is semantically similar to n_1. n_1 and n_2 are considered semantically similar if their similarity is above a threshold θ (θ=0.80 for high similarity). However, the two operations choose the noun phrases for replacement based on different criteria. Also, both these operations will replace n_1 with n_2 (REPLACEABLE(n_1, n_2)) based on the following constraints: (i) n_2 does not occur in the sentence containing n_1, (ii) n_1 and n_2 have the same plurality, (iii) n_1 and n_2 have the same number of noun terms. After n_1 is replaced by n_2, a corrective operation is performed - if n_1 is preceded by 'a' or 'an', then it is changed to suit n_2.

Next, we describe the experimental setup and the analysis of results.

5   Experimental Setup

This section presents the experimental design for testing the effectiveness of our approach. Our validation experiments are as follows:

1. **Statistical analysis** - validates the statistical significance of the improvements in cohesion and coherence of automatically generated believable fake text over the fake text.

2. **Believability test** - validates the following via human subjects: Does applying the believability module generate believable fake texts that have lower probability of being discerned than fake text?

Data: We randomly selected 25 technical articles from Communications of the ACM - a leading technical magazine. Based on the selected articles, we generated 3 sets of text documents. Each set contains 25 text documents as follows:

- *Legit text set* - First, we randomly extracted two to three consecutive paragraphs from each of the 25 original articles and created legit texts belonging to this set. The purpose of extraction is to limit the size of the documents in this set to keep it comparable to the size of context modified by the believability module.

- *Fake text set* - Next, using our fake generation module we identified the most salient sentence s_i in the original article. We also identified the context $c(s_i)$ (length of the context ($2x$) = 10) surrounding the salient sentence. Subsequently, we generated fake documents by extracting paragraphs containing $c(s_i)$ but without the salient sentence s_i.

	Fake text		Believable fake text		*p*-value
	Mean	SD	Mean	SD	
Cohesion	0.24	0.09	0.26	0.06	0.026
Coherence	0.37	0.10	0.40	0.09	0.013

Table 1: Comparing the change in cohesion and coherence of the fake and the believable fake texts.

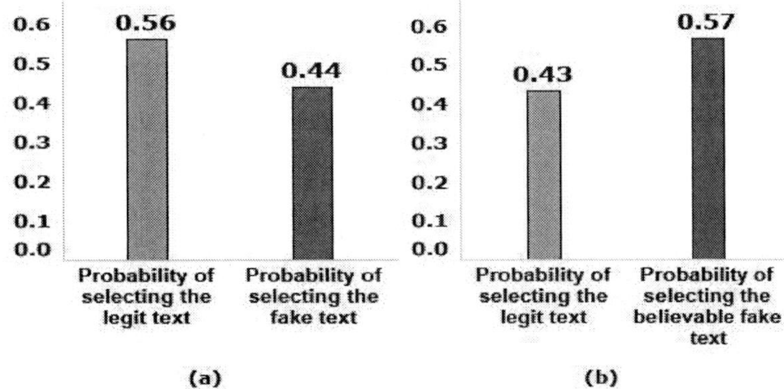

Figure 1: Aggregated analysis of 625 responses per test case of selecting the text perceived as legit - (a) given a pair of legit and fake texts (left), and (b) given a pair of legit and believable fake texts (right).

- *Believable fake text set* - Finally, we generated this set by improving the cohesion and coherence of the texts in the fake text set using our believability module.

The aforementioned method to generate sets of documents is suitable as it helps keep the legit text, fake text, and believable fake texts comparable. These texts are all extractions and modifications of consecutive paragraphs from the same original article, having the same topicality, reading level, and sharing the writing style of the same author(s).

6 Experiments and Results

This section details the experiments performed and their results.

Statistical analysis - For validating the statistical significance of the change in cohesion and coherence measures, we used the two-tailed paired t-test. We compared the 25 pairs of fake and their corresponding believable fake texts based on their cohesion and coherence measures. The results are as shown in Table 1. Looking at the *p*-values in the table, we can observe a statistically significant improvement in the cohesion and coherence of the text due to the operations in the believability module.

Believability test - This is a well-defined test in the domain of cyber deception that is used to test and measure the believability of a fake object. A perfectly believable fake text is one that is indistinguishable in comparison to a legit text (Bowen et al., 2009). Bowen et al. (2009) have described the procedure to conduct a believability test as follows: i) Choose two texts such that one is the believable fake text for which we wish to measure its believability and the second is chosen at random from a set of legit texts. ii) Select a human subject at random to participate in a user study. iii) Show the human subject the texts chosen in step one and ask them to decide which of the two texts is the legit text. A perfectly believable fake text is chosen with a probability greater than or equal to 50% (an outcome that would be achieved if the human subject decided completely at random).

In order to observe the change in believability due to the operations in the believability module, we conducted two types of believability tests. For the first type, we compared 25 pairs of believable fake and its corresponding legit texts derived from the same original article. We then conducted the second type of believability test where we compared 25 pairs of fake and its corresponding legit texts derived from

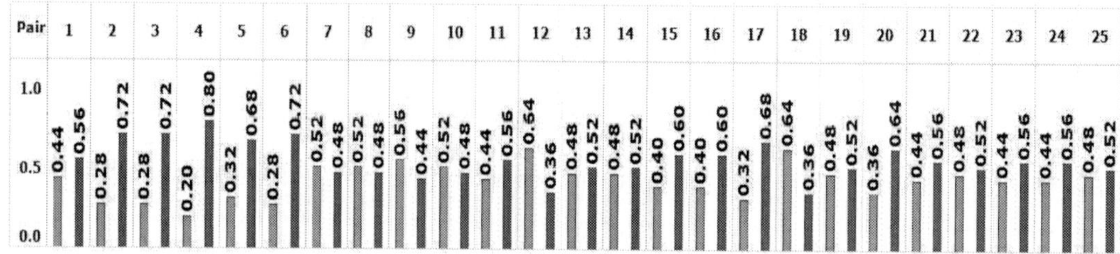

Figure 2: Distribution per test pair for 25 human subjects, where the orange bar (left) for each pair indicates the probability of identifying the legit text and blue bar (right) indicates the probability of selecting the believable fake text as the legit text.

the same original article. We did not inform the subjects about the difference in the pairs apriori. We showed each of the 50 pairs to 25 human subjects and asked them to identify the legit text. The human subjects were recruited through classes in our university and through a crowdsourcing platform (the highest trusted 'level 3' contributor set on *Figure-Eight platform*[2]). In total, we received 1250 responses for selecting the legit text in each of the 50 pairs.

We evaluated the 1250 responses using the believability test's performance metric - the probability of selecting a fake or believable fake text as the legit text. Figure 1 shows the aggregated analysis of all the 625 responses per type of believability test. Figure 1(a) shows the probability of a subject selecting the fake text as a legit text to be only 44% (p-value: 0.037, two-tailed t-test), indicating that the subjects were able to discern the legit text correctly for a statistically significant number of times. This probability indicates the likelihood of a distinguishing factor in the text that helped the subjects to identify the fake text. On the other hand, figure 1(b) shows a probability of 57% (p-value: 0.006, two-tailed t-test) for selecting a believable fake text as a legit text. This result implies that the believable fake text is truly believable for the subjects, and there may not exist a distinguishing factor that helped the subjects to recognize the believable fake text as fake.

We further performed a fine-grained analysis to validate our hypothesis that an increase in the cohesion and coherence of text would improve the believability of the text. For this analysis, we compared the individual probability of selecting a believable fake text in a believable fake-legit text pair for each of the 25 pairs. The results are as shown in figure 2. We found that 76% of the tests resulted in greater than 50% probability for a subject to identify the believable fake text as legit. These results indicate the positive effect of applying our believability module on the believability perception of fake text.

6.1 Limitations and Error Analysis

Our believability module is dependent on a semantic similarity model to provide us the similarity of noun phrases. Measuring text similarity and alignment for comparing the meaning are challenging tasks and open research questions. We chose UMBC-EBIQUITY-CORE because its similarity computation is based on leveraging both distributed semantics (Latent Semantic Analysis) and semantic networks (WordNet) for generalization. However, errors in the chosen model influences the performance of the believability module to have fewer choices when substituting similar noun phrases. Also, our approach is dependent on the POS tagger to identify noun phrases. If the tagger fails to annotate a noun or its plural form accurately, then the identified candidates for substitution would not be the complete set of nouns occurring in the document. These limitations can reduce the number of possible substitutions and therefore, limiting the possible improvements in the cohesion and coherence of the fake text.

We also conducted an error analysis on the results of the believability test to understand the characteristics of text that was not perceived as legit. In figure 2, out of the 25 pairs of believable fake-legit texts, six pairs were such that the legit text was discerned. This could be a result of pre-existing complexity in comprehending the text that was randomly chosen for generating the believable fake text. The characteristics of hard to comprehend text includes a greater presence of infrequently used words and longer

---

[2]https://www.figure-eight.com/

sentences. For instance, among the six pairs, we found sentences containing nearly 40 words in the chosen text. These observations motivate our future work to improve the believability by also incorporating other features of text comprehension that are beyond cohesion and coherence alone.

7   Conclusion and Future Work

We designed a novel computational linguistics method to enhance the believability of fake texts, which are used in cybersecurity solutions to deceive cyber attackers. Our methods rely on improving the linguistic consistency by increasing cohesion 1) at the sentence level via coreference correction between sentences, and 2) at the paragraph level via semantic relatedness among entities. We evaluated the outcome of our method using statistical techniques to measure the significance of improvements in the cohesion, coherence, and believability of the generated text. We found that the increase in the values of cohesion and coherence metrics for the believable fake text was statistically significant when compared with the fake text. Further, the believability test showed that the probability to distinguish a legit text from a believable fake text is lower than the probability to distinguish a legit text from a fake text. These results prove our hypothesis that the computer-generated fake text with higher cohesion and coherence leads to improvement in the believability of the text. These results further indicate the effectiveness of our method in generating believable fake text for misleading potential cyber attackers and increasing the cost of intellectual property thefts.

For the purpose of reproducibility, our dataset will be available upon request, for research purposes. Our future work will explore an extension of the newly developed methods to analyze and address the challenge of obscuring salient information at multiple locations in a given text. We will also experiment with varied types of documents by domain including non-technical documents. The application of our methods will help to create benchmark data repositories of both legit and fake text documents for cyber deception research.

8   Acknowledgement

This work was partially supported by the Office of Naval Research grants N00014-16-1-2896 and N00014-18-1-2670.

References

Mohammed H Almeshekah and Eugene H Spafford. 2016. Cyber security deception. In *Cyber Deception*, pages 23–50. Springer.

Brian M Bowen, Shlomo Hershkop, Angelos D Keromytis, and Salvatore J Stolfo. 2009. Baiting inside attackers using decoy documents. In *International Conference on Security and Privacy in Communication Systems*, pages 51–70. Springer.

Jill Burstein, Joel Tetreault, and Slava Andreyev. 2010. Using entity-based features to model coherence in student essays. In *Human language technologies: The 2010 annual conference of the North American chapter of the Association for Computational Linguistics*, pages 681–684. Association for Computational Linguistics.

Scott A Crossley, Kristopher Kyle, and Danielle S McNamara. 2016. The tool for the automatic analysis of text cohesion (taaco): Automatic assessment of local, global, and text cohesion. *Behavior research methods*, 48(4):1227–1237.

Scott Deerwester, Susan T Dumais, George W Furnas, Thomas K Landauer, and Richard Harshman. 1990. Indexing by latent semantic analysis. *Journal of the American society for information science*, 41(6):391.

Gunes Erkan and Dragomir R Radev. 2004. Lexrank: Graph-based lexical centrality as salience in text summarization. *Journal of Artificial Intelligence Research*, 22:457–479.

Lushan Han, Abhay L Kashyap, Tim Finin, James Mayfield, and Jonathan Weese. 2013. Umbc_ebiquity-core: semantic textual similarity systems. In *Second Joint Conference on Lexical and Computational Semantics (* SEM), Proceedings of the Main Conference and the Shared Task: Semantic Textual Similarity*, volume 1, pages 44–52. Association for Computational Linguistics.

Kristin E Heckman, Frank J Stech, Roshan K Thomas, Ben Schmoker, and Alexander W Tsow. 2015. *Cyber denial, deception and counter deception*. Springer.

Sushil Jajodia, VS Subrahmanian, Vipin Swarup, and Cliff Wang. 2016. *Cyber Deception*. Springer.

Mirella Lapata and Regina Barzilay. 2005. Automatic evaluation of text coherence: Models and representations. In *IJCAI*, volume 5, pages 1085–1090. ACM.

Ziheng Lin, Hwee Tou Ng, and Min-Yen Kan. 2011. Automatically evaluating text coherence using discourse relations. In *Proceedings of the 49th Annual Meeting of the Association for Computational Linguistics: Human Language Technologies-Volume 1*, pages 997–1006. Association for Computational Linguistics.

Inderjeet Mani, Barbara Gates, and Eric Bloedorn. 1999. Improving summaries by revising them. In *Proceedings of the 37th annual meeting of the Association for Computational Linguistics on Computational Linguistics*, pages 558–565. Association for Computational Linguistics.

Danielle S McNamara and Walter Kintsch. 1996. Learning from texts: Effects of prior knowledge and text coherence. *Discourse processes*, 22(3):247–288.

Danielle S McNamara, Arthur C Graesser, Philip M McCarthy, and Zhiqiang Cai. 2014. *Automated evaluation of text and discourse with Coh-Metrix*. Cambridge University Press.

Rada Mihalcea, Courtney Corley, and Carlo Strapparava. 2006. Corpus-based and knowledge-based measures of text semantic similarity. In *Proceedings of the 21st national conference on Artificial intelligence*, volume 1, pages 775–780.

Eleni Miltsakaki and Karen Kukich. 2000. Automated evaluation of coherence in student essays. In *Proceedings of LREC 2000*, pages 1–8. LREC.

Shashi Narayan. 2014. *Generating and Simplifying Sentences*. Ph.D. thesis, Universite de Lorraine.

Ani Nenkova and Kathleen McKeown. 2012. A survey of text summarization techniques. In *Mining text data*, pages 43–76. Springer.

Jose Otero and Walter Kintsch. 1992. Failures to detect contradictions in a text: What readers believe versus what they read. *Psychological Science*, 3(4):229–236.

Sampsa Rauti and Ville Leppanen. 2017. A survey on fake entities as a method to detect and monitor malicious activity. In *2017 25th Euromicro International Conference on Parallel, Distributed and Network-based Processing (PDP)*, pages 386–390. IEEE.

Neil C Rowe and Julian Rrushi. 2016. *Introduction to Cyberdeception*. Springer.

Asaf Shabtai, Maya Bercovitch, Lior Rokach, Ya'akov Kobi Gal, Yuval Elovici, and Erez Shmueli. 2016. Behavioral study of users when interacting with active honeytokens. *ACM Transactions on Information and System Security (TISSEC)*, 18(3):9:1–21.

Advaith Siddharthan, Ani Nenkova, and Kathleen McKeown. 2011. Information status distinctions and referring expressions: An empirical study of references to people in news summaries. *Computational Linguistics*, 37(4):811–842.

Advaith Siddharthan. 2006. Syntactic simplification and text cohesion. *Research on Language and Computation*, 4(1):77–109.

Jonathan Voris, Nathaniel Boggs, and Salvatore J Stolfo. 2012. Lost in translation: Improving decoy documents via automated translation. In *Security and Privacy Workshops (SPW), 2012 IEEE Symposium on*, pages 129–133. IEEE.

Jonathan Voris, Jill Jermyn, Angelos D Keromytis, and Salvatore J Stolfo. 2013. Bait and snitch: Defending computer systems with decoys. In *Cyber Infrastructure Protection Conference*, pages 1–25. United states army college press.

Ben Whitham, Tim Turner, and Lawrie Brown. 2015. Automated processes for evaluating the realism of high-interaction honeyfiles. In *Proceedings of the 14th European Conference on Cyber Warfare and Security*, pages 307–316. Academic Conferences International Limited.

Ben Whitham. 2017. Automating the generation of enticing text content for high-interaction honeyfiles. In *Proceedings of the 50th Hawaii International Conference on System Sciences*, pages 6069–6078. HICSS.

Addressing the Winograd Schema Challenge as a Sequence Ranking Task

Juri Opitz and **Anette Frank**
Research Training Group AIPHES,
Leibniz ScienceCampus "Empirical Linguistics and Computational Language Modeling"
Department for Computational Linguistics
69120 Heidelberg
{opitz,frank}@cl.uni-heidelberg.de

Abstract

The Winograd Schema Challenge targets pronominal anaphora resolution problems which require the application of cognitive inference in combination with world knowledge. These problems are easy to solve for humans but most difficult to solve for machines. Computational models that previously addressed this task rely on syntactic preprocessing and incorporation of external knowledge by manually crafted features. We address the Winograd Schema Challenge from a new perspective as a *sequence ranking task*, and design a Siamese neural sequence ranking model which performs significantly better than a random baseline, even when *solely* trained on sequences of words. We evaluate against a baseline and a state-of-the-art system on two data sets and show that anonymization of noun phrase candidates strongly helps our model to generalize.

1 Introduction

The Winograd Schema Challenge (WSC) targets difficult pronoun resolution problems which are easy to resolve for humans, but represent a great challenge for AI systems because they require the application of cognitive inferencing in combination with world knowledge (Levesque et al., 2012; Levesque, 2014). It has been argued that a computer that is able to solve WS problems with human-like accuracy must be able to perform "human-like" reasoning and that the WSC can be seen as an alternative to the Turing test. Consider the following Winograd Schema (WS):

Example 1.1 *The city councilmen* refused *the demonstrators* a permit because *they* feared violence.

Both *city councilmen* and *demonstrators* agree in number and gender and even in semantic type, as both mentions refer to groups of humans (with political interests). While we could imagine a city with councilmen who approve violence and hence forbid a demonstration by peaceful protesters, this reading may appear nonsensical to most readers. Most humans will straightforwardly resolve the pronoun *they* to corefer with *the city councilmen*. Now consider the outcome of replacing a single word – the predicate *feared* – with the semantically related predicate *advocated*, yielding its *twin* sentence:

Example 1.2 *The city councilmen* refused *the demonstrators* a permit because *they* advocated violence.

With this change, the resolution is reversed: now *they* refers to *the demonstrators*. Humans may reason that city council men are naturally concerned with the well-being of their city and thus *they* are not in favor of a demonstration by protesters who advocate violence. Winograd problems as displayed in Examples 1.1 and 1.2 occur very rarely in natural language texts and cannot be properly resolved by traditional coreference resolution (CR) systems. The primary reason is that standard CR systems heavily rely on features such as gender or number agreement or mention-distance information. However, such features do not give away any knowledge that would be useful for resolving WS problems. Given a random baseline of 0.5 accuracy, the Stanford resolver (Lee et al.,), winner of the CoNLL 2011 Shared Task (Pradhan et al., 2011), achieves a sobering accuracy of 0.53 when facing Winograd Schema problems (Rahman and Ng, 2012). Lee et al. (2017) describe a state-of-the-art neural system for general neural coreference resolution and observe that, while trained on much more data than is available in

Proceedings of the First International Workshop on Language Cognition and Computational Models, pages 41–52
Santa Fe, New Mexico, United States, August 20, 2018.
https://doi.org/10.18653/v1/P17

the WSC, their system shows little advance in the uphill battle of resolving hard pronoun coreference problems that require world knowledge.

As our main contribution we are proposing a novel and very general take on the WSC task that we formulate as a *sequence ranking task* in a *neural Siamese sequence ranking model*. Moreover, we design *features derived from manually designed knowledge bases* and show how they can be integrated in this model. We investigate *anonymization of noun phrase candidates* that significantly enhances the generalization capacity of the model. We evaluate against baselines and a state-of-the-art (SOTA) system with special focus on the impact of different features and *propose connotation frames* as a novel feature for the WSC task. All Siamese model variants, even those trained on word sequences only, show significant improvements over the baseline on our main testing set. Our best performing model achieves 0.63 accuracy.

2   WSC Datasets and Related Work

Strict Data is Scarce: WSCL. Starting with the work by Levesque et al. (2012), a collection of (currently) 282 *strict* WS problems is maintained online[1], which will henceforth be referred to as WSCL. We make a distinction between *strict* and *relaxed* Winograd Schemata. Relaxed Winograd Schemata are problems which can be solved by computing simple corpus statistics. E.g., *The chimpanzee couldn't use Linux because it is an animal* is of the relaxed type because a simple google query returns significantly more results for *chimpanzee is an animal* than *Linux is an animal* (19,700 vs. 3 hits). Such relaxed, easy-to-solve examples are not contained in the WSCL data set, but do occur in the WSCR data set, described below. The problems in WSCL have an average length of 18 tokens. Some problems may consist of more than one sentence and require understanding across sentence boundaries.[2]

Relaxed Data: WSCR. The main dataset used in this work[3], which we refer to as WSCR, was published by Rahman and Ng (2012). The data was created by 30 undergraduate students. It comprises 943 twin sentences and comes already divided into training (70%) and test set (30%). As opposed to the WSCL data, WSCR comprises both strict and relaxed Winograd schemata. We found that it also contains sentences with no straightforward resolution, as in Ex. 2.1 and 2.2 (with gold antecedents underlined):

Example 2.1 ***Bob*** *likes to play with* ***Jimbo*** *because* ***he*** *loves playing.*

Example 2.2 ***The bus driver*** *yelled at* ***the kid*** *after* ***she*** *drove her vehicle.*

When we presented these problems to a class of students, close to half of them voted for the other reading in Example 2.1 (more than half in Example 2.2). This is reasonable, since the alternative reading (Jimbo loves playing) can be inferred from the fact that generally people like to play with someone who likes to play – rather than with someone who does not like to play. The alternative reading of Example 2.2 could be even more likely, since it makes perfect sense that when a kid tries to drive the bus driver's vehicle, the bus driver will get angry and might yell at the kid. When inspecting the data, we found that while notably having lower quality than WSCL, most sentences have a clearly preferred reading, which coheres with the gold annotation. The problems in WSCR seem less diverse as all consist of exactly one sentence and in every sentence we find at least one discourse connector or a comma connecting a main clause with the antecedent candidates to a sub-clause that contains the pronoun.

Feature- and Example-based Ranking. Together with the WSCR data set, Rahman and Ng (2012) also publicized the description of a linear ranking system that achieves 73% accuracy on the published data. The system relies on 8 features, which it uses to fit a SVM ranking model. Contrary to our work, all features depend on syntactic dependency annotation. While incorporating complex external knowledge resources such as FrameNet (Baker et al., 1998) or narrative chains (Chambers and Jurafsky, 2008), the most helpful feature turned out to be simple Google-queries, it significantly outperformed the random baseline with a considerable margin of 6% to the next best single feature. Kruengkrai et al. (2014) attempted to replicate parts of the system, selecting five features. Some of them were implemented

---

[1] https://cs.nyu.edu/faculty/davise/papers/WinogradSchemas/WSCollection.xml

[2] E.g. *It was a summer afternoon, and* ***the dog*** *was sitting in the middle of the lawn. After a while, it got up and moved to* ***a spot under the tree***, *because* ***it*** *was hot.*

[3] url: http://www.hlt.utdallas.edu/~vince/papers/emnlp12.html

differently, e.g. instead of querying Google directly, the Google n-gram dataset (Brants and Franz, 2006) was used. The authors present a system that extracts representative examples from the web. Both systems were tested on a subset of the WSCR test set (for the problems where web examples were found). The reimplemented system yielded 0.56 accuracy while their own approach yielded 0.69 accuracy.

Integer Linear Program (ILP). Peng et al. (2015b) use an ILP (Schrijver, 1986) inference approach with a novel way of knowledge representation. Their system yields 0.76 accuracy on WSCR, which is the current state-of-the-art result on this data. In their approach "Predicate Schemas" are instantiated and scored using knowledge acquired from external knowledge bases compiled into constraints for a decision. Consider 'The bee landed on the flower because **it** {was hungry, had pollen}', where the gold resolution is that (i) *the bee was hungry* and (ii) *the flower had pollen*. A simple predicate schema for this problem is instantiated as $hungry(bee)$ vs. $hungry(flower)$ and $has\,pollen(flower)$ vs. $has\,pollen(bee)$. Scores for the instantiated predicates are then gathered from external knowledge sources such as Google[4].

Other Work on Difficult Coreference Resolution. Sharma et al. (2015) build a semantic parser and Schüller (2014) use syntactic dependency annotation and knowledge base linking in order to solve WSC problems. Both works use the Answer Set Programming language (ASP, cf. (Baral, 2003; Gelfond and Lifschitz, 1988)) on the generated abstract representations for reasoning about the correct antecedent. Sharma et al. (2015) for evaluation considers only causal attributive and direct causal events and Schüller (2014) performs experiments with only 4 twin problems for demonstration purposes.

We conclude that (i) all examined prior work focuses on either a specific subset of Winograd problems or/and is tested on only one specific data set, WSCL or WSCR but never both. Also (ii) we are the first to present an end-to-end WSC system which, contrary to all prior methods, does not rely on sophisticated preprocessing or linguistic annotation. (iii) We avoid heavy reliance on Google searches, which we argue the approaches of both Rahman and Ng (2012) and Peng et al. (2015b) suffer from. This is mainly due to two reasons: 1., Google has restricted automatic access to their search engine, making it difficult to solve more than a handful of pronoun resolution problems in short time without payment and, even more importantly 2., reproduction of results is impossible due to the nature of Google's search-algorithm as a black box – one cannot ensure to retrieve the exact same or even similar query results as previous authors. Our work, by contrast, does not rely on non-reproducible features and will be the first to present an end-to-end neural approach for addressing the WSC.

3 Framing the WSC as a Sequence Ranking Task

We propose a new view on Winograd problems by translating the problem to a sequence ranking or classification task that discriminates a preferred or plausible sentence reading from a very similar but dispreferred or implausible reading. The preferred reading emerges when we replace the pronoun with its coreferent gold antecedent noun phrase and the dispreferred reading emerges when we instead use the wrong antecedent as the replacement. For example, given the WS problem *Joe paid the detective after he received the final report on the case.*, we can derive the preferred reading:

Example 3.1 *Joe paid **the detective** after **Joe** received the final report on the case.*

and the clearly less preferred reading

Example 3.2 *Joe paid **the detective** after **the detective** received the final report on the case.*

Most humans easily come to understand that Example 3.1 is in line with common sense (preferred), while the second Example 3.2 seems somewhat bogus and less in line with common sense (dispreferred). Inserting the correct (incorrect) antecedent noun phrase in place of the pronoun converts a Winograd problem with alternative but clear pronoun resolutions into preferred and dispreferred readings.

Formal Description. Let a Winograd problem be defined as a tuple $(s, p, c^+, c^-) \in W$, where s is a sequence of tokens, p is the given anaphoric pronominal token and c^+ represents the correct and c^- the incorrect noun phrase antecedent. We design a function $f : W \to W'$, returning a tuple $(r^+, r^-) \in W'$, containing two sequences of tokens, where r^+ is the preferred reading of s and r^- is the dispreferred reading of s which are the result of replacing the anaphoric pronoun p in s with c^+ or c^-.[5]

---

[4]Note that *plants* and *bees* are both very likely to have pollen, the predicate schema may be prone to errors in this case.

[5]When the pronouns are possessive (his, her, their), we replace p in s with the genitive form of c^+ or c^-.

Discussion. We derive sentences without pronouns from sentences with pronouns by inserting the aforementioned corresponding noun. A motivation for this process is the assumption that pronouns 'stand for', 'replace' or are 'substitutes' for previously mentioned or understood noun phrases. Framing the problem as a sequence preference ranking task has two major advantages. First, by replacing the anaphor with one of the possible antecedents, we contextualize each of these candidates to the local context of the anaphor. This contextualization can be exploited in a neural end-to-end system that constructs a full sentence representation, including the (resolved) pronoun. Second, with the two alternative readings being constructed, we can define a model that determines which of the two readings is preferred, or can be considered more plausible. That is, we frame the task as a preference ranking task, as opposed to a categorical binary classification task. In sum, we argue that framing/formulating the task of Winograd sentence/problem resolution as a task of *comparing the plausibility of alternative readings* provides an appealing alternative to prior task formulations: It permits the application of hypothetically any type of sentence representation model to be applied out-of-the-box.

Note however that by no means we want to postulate that humans understand and resolve Winograd problems by internally comparing a pair of complete sentence representations with alternatively resolved pronouns. But what perhaps is also clear is that humans do not dependency parse the full sentence and then access knowledge bases weighting manually crafted mention features as commonly done in the WSC task (Rahman and Ng, 2012; Sharma et al., 2015).

4 Neural Sequence Models for the WSC

Having converted each WS problem into two highly similar yet different readings allows us to define a neural end-to-end model in at least two different ways. In a naïve formulation (**Naïve Model**), we can simply force a model to predict whether a specific reading is plausible or implausible (binary classification). Alternatively, we can also exploit the fact that the two readings – produced by replacing the anaphor with a candidate antecedent (see above) – are highly similarand frame the task as a sequence ranking problem and design a *relational* model that constructs two internal representations that are compared and ranked. We call this the **Siamese Model**.

Naïve Model. We encode a sequence of tokens with an embedding layer and a two-layered Bi-LSTM (Hochreiter and Schmidhuber, 1997) and use a logistic regression layer on top to predict whether the sentence – representing one or the other of the two possible readings – is accepted or not. For training, from each pair of readings indexed by $i = 1, ..., N$ we extract two training examples, where the preferred reading r_i^+ is assigned class 1, and the dispreferred reading r_i^- is assigned class 0. This model can be optimized by minimizing a standard binary cross-entropy loss. A disadvantage of this model is that the classifier is not explicitly optimized towards the goal of discriminating competing readings since during training accepted and inaccepted readings are isolated from each other.

Siamese Model. Similar to the Naïve Model, we encode a sequence of tokens with an embedding layer followed by two-layered Bi-LSTM and use a single SELU (Klambauer et al., 2017) unit on top that predicts a plausibility score $h_\theta(r)$ for a reading r, where θ are the parameters of the model. The model is mirrored and uses shared weights to process two different representations at the same time, one for each reading (Fig. 1). We compute two plausibility scores over a pair of readings for every training example, where the aim is to maximize the difference between the scores for the plausible sequences and the implausible ones. At inference, the resolution with highest plausibility score is chosen. We avoid decomposing a pair of readings into two independent training and testing examples as done in the naïve model and by feeding the model both sequences at the same time we directly optimize the model to assign the preferred reading a higher plausibility score compared to the dispreferred reading. This is reflected in the (totally differentiable) margin ranking loss, which we define as

$$\frac{1}{N} \sum_{i=1}^{N} \left[1 - \sigma\big(h_\theta(r_i^+) - h_\theta(r_i^-)\big) \right], \tag{1}$$

where σ is the logistic function. The general architecture is outlined in Fig. 1 and lends itself naturally to the incorporation of at least two different types of additional input features.

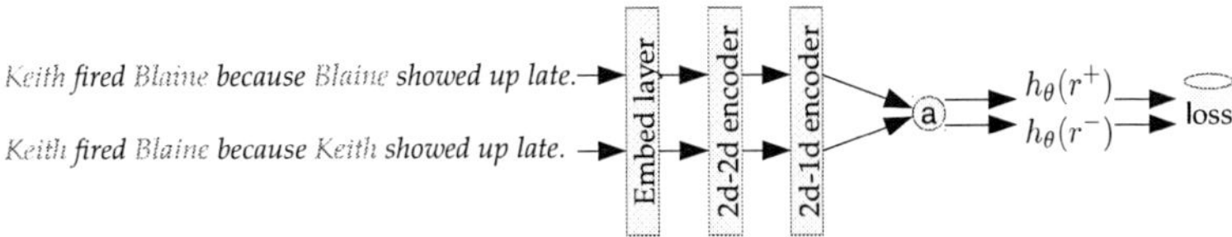

Figure 1: General Siamese architecture for comparing WSC readings. Embed layer is a function converting a sequence of tokens to a sequence of real valued vectors (we use a lookup table containing pretrained GloVe embeddings). 2d-2d encoder means any function that converts a sequence of vectors into another sequence of vectors (we use a Bi-LSTM returning state vectors). 2d-1d means any encoder converting a sequence of vectors into a single vector (we use a Bi-LSTM and concatenate the end states of each sequential read). 'a' can represent any activation neuron (we use a SELU unit).

Siamese Multi-Input Model. Our general architecture is displayed in Figure 1. The architecture naturally lends itself for the incorporation of many additional features, which have the potential to provide pointed world knowledge for the model that it cannot derive from the scarce training data. In the basic model (Figure 1), we can inject two additional types of features: real valued vectors and real valued matrices. Consider that the word embedding sequence for a Winograd example is of length l which is again projected by a Bi-LSTM (2d-2d encoder in Figure 1) onto a state matrix of dimension $l \times n$ and consider the case of one additional matrix type feature: after the matrix has been shaped to the same dimensionality $l \times n$ we can use concatenation, element-wise addition and element-wise multiplication to merge the additional feature representation with the sentence representation into a representation of dimension $l \times 4n$ before it is fed into the next layer. As additional matrix-type features we experiment with dependency edge sequences and information about the connotation of the arguments induced by their predicate as stated in the resource *Connotation Frames* (Rashkin et al., 2015; Rashkin et al., 2016). The features and motivation for usage are more extensively discussed in the next paragraphs.

We can also incorporate features which come as real valued vectors: we use an averaged semantic embedding of the tokens of the candidate noun phrase (described more closely in the next paragraph) to provide useful information for cases where the candidate noun phrase is not a generic person name but carries meaning. The vector can be injected into the model between the 2d-1d encoder and the output activation computation. A FF-layer is used to shape the vector so that it matches the output dimension h of the 2d-1d encoder enabling us to perform element-wise addition, element-wise multiplication and concatenation resulting in a high level sentence representation of dimension $4h$.

Anonymization of Candidate NPs. The fact that training data is really small motivates us to propose anonymization of noun phrase candidates as a simple means for discouraging the model to memorize the noun phrase candidates, forcing it to focus on the complex but general interactions between arguments and predicates. Consider the following pair (correct antecedents underlined):

Example 4.1 *Mary thanked Susan for all the help she had received.*

Example 4.2 *Mary thanked Susan for all the help she had given.*

Memorizing the candidates would be fatal for any model, since the resolution is not determined by the candidate noun phrases alone (both are generic names of the same gender), but rather from the interaction between predicates and arguments. We want the model to focus on deeper information from the meaning of the sentences that is general and relevant to support the correct resolution of the pronoun.

Candidate NP-level Feature. While many WS problems can be easily solved by humans in anonymized form, there are cases for which information about the candidate noun phrases is necessary, or even mandatory, especially for the relaxed Winograd problems in the WSCR-data. Consider

Example 4.3 *He hates Cuba and likes Japan because it is a communist country.*

This example is not strict because it is rather easy to resolve for machines by simply computing similarity measures between the candidate noun phrases and the predicate *communist country*.[6] ConceptNet (Speer and Havasi, 2012) and the available semantic embeddings trained on this resource (Speer and Lowry-Duda, 2017) i.a. contain information from WordNet (Miller, 1995) and may give the model the

---

[6]More precisely, the predicate *communist country* restricts the arguments unambiguously to the correct phrase.

```
S: (n) Cuba, Republic of Cuba (a communist state in the Caribbean on the island of
   Cuba)
S: (n) Cuba (the largest island in the West Indies)
```

Figure 2: WordNet gloss for the noun *Cuba*. It contains information about the political stance of the government.

	The	ball	hit	the	window	and	Bill	fixed	the	it.
p(wx)		-0.33			-0.20		0.33			-0.03
p(rx)		0.06			-0.73		0.13			0.40
e(x)		-0.20			0.33		0.60			0.73

Figure 3: An example of how we apply Connotation Frames for *hit* and *fix*. The numerical value $\in [-1, 1]$ ranges from positive (+1) to negative (-1). p(wx) and p(rx) represent the perspective of the writer (w) or reader (r) towards the object or subject of the verb x. e(x) stands for the effect on the subject or object. The frames contain 4 more perspectives which are omitted in the Figure.

information that *Cuba* is a communist country (see Figure 2). The information from the gloss that Cuba is the largest island in the West Indies is not necessary, but one could easily make up a WS problem for which it is necessary as in *He likes Cuba and hates Japan because it is located in the Caribbean Sea.*. This is the only feature acting on a candidate noun phrase level and it is computed by averaging the semantic embeddings of the corresponding tokenized candidate noun phrases.

Dependency Edges. For the resolution of many WS problems, feeding explicit syntactic information may be useful and help the model in learning useful information about predicates and their interactions. Consider Examples 4.1 and 4.2, where the predicate of the pronoun is *gives(x,help)* and the predicate in which both possible antecedents participate in is *thanks(Mary,Susan)*. It is very useful to know that Mary is the subject of *thanks* and Susan the object. When provided with such information the model may learn the abstract pattern that the subject argument of *gives* is more likely to be the object of *thank(x,y)* than its subject, while the subject argument of *receive* is more likely to be the subject argument of *thank(x,y)*.

Connotation Frames. *Connotation Frames* is a resource[7] that contains frames of verbs that indicate how the arguments of the verb are affected by the predicate meaning (Rashkin et al., 2015; Rashkin et al., 2016). The frames represent this information by presenting numerical values for seven types of connotations concerning different components of the frame. For example, the value of the object of the frame *resolve(s,o)* is negatively connotated. This reflects that what needs be to resolved is usually considered a problem, and a problem is most likely an issue which is perceived negatively. Consider

Example 4.4 *The ball* hit *the window* and Bill *fixed* it.

For application we retrieve the frames for *hit* and *fix* and apply them to the arguments of the respective verbs in a sentence, resulting in a matrix with columns of dimension seven. The result is displayed in Figure 3 (where only 3 dimensions are displayed). For words or arguments of predicates not covered by the resource, we use a zero-vector.

5 Experiments

Data. Unlike most other research on WSC, we test our models on both data sets discussed above – WSCL, the smaller data set of higher quality (282 examples) with strict and mostly unambiguous WSC cases, which we exclusively use for testing and WSCR, which comes in a predefined split of 1322 training and 564 testing problems, but which is of slightly reduced quality for the reasons discussed in Section 3. Note that, as in previous work, we do not exploit the fact that each Winograd problem has a twin.

Baselines. Given that the WS problems in WSCL and WSCR come in pairs with alternative resolutions to first vs. second antecedent candidate, we apply a random process as the baseline with 0.5 probability of achieving the correct guess. Since the problem can be seen as a binary classification task, we calculate binomial tests to assess the probability of the zero-hypothesis that a random process achieves the same

---

[7]Available at `https://homes.cs.washington.edu/~hrashkin/connframe.html`.

amount or more correct predictions than the evaluated system. We also downloaded the state of the art system of Peng et al. (2015a), which the authors made publicly available[8]. However, it is important to note that the publicized system had been retrained on both training and testing data of WSCR[9], making it difficult to re-evaluate it under the original experimental conditions. When evaluating the system with anonymized candidates, we only select cases where the integrated mention detection was able to detect both (and only both) candidates and linked the pronoun to one of those. All other cases we have to treat as unresolved. The downloaded system yields an accuracy of 0.99 (397 correct, 3 incorrect, 164 unresolved) on WSCR. In our evaluation Table we present the result from their paper (Table 1: *SOTA*) As an additional baseline we use as a representation of the input sentences the representations predicted by a trained *sentence embedding model*, here *InferSent* (Conneau et al., 2017). InferSent has been been trained on large-scale natural language inference tasks (Bowman et al., 2015) and therefore may have internalized valuable information about whether sentence readings are coherent or rather nonsensical. We infer 4096-dimensional sentence vectors with the trained model provided by the authors[10] and fit a linear ranker SVM, using randomly sampled development data to find a suitable regularization parameter.

Experimental Setup and Evaluation. We evaluate our models in two testing scenarios: (i) *Train:*WSCR+*Test:*WSCL*:* In this setup we train the model on the full WSCR data and test on the unseen WSCL data, to test the generalization capability of our models across data sets. (ii) *Train+Test:*WSCR In the second scenario we use the predefined split of the WSCR data for training and evaluation. Since both scenarios do not involve a development set, we randomly split off 100 twin pair problems (200 examples) from the training data for development purposes. Since there is much stochasticity in the models (stochastic gradient descent, parameter sampling, training-development split, etc.), we do five random initializations with different seeds. We choose the model parameterizations from the epochs where they performed best on the development set. These models predict the test set and we compute mean and standard deviation of accuracy. We also introduce two ensembles, the naïve ensemble (NaïveE) and the Siamese ensemble (SiamE), which are majority voters informed by the predictions of the five different random seed models.

Parameter Search. We examine the Naïve model and the Siamese model, using all discussed features and pretrained, fixed 300 dimensional GloVe word embeddings (Pennington et al., 2014). Dependency edge embeddings with 10 dimensions are initialized randomly from $\mathcal{N}_{10}(0, 1)$. The two embeddings for the anonymized mentions are drawn from $\mathcal{N}_{300}(0, 1)$. The Bi-LSTMs have 32 hidden units each, the weight matrix used for the linear transformation of the inputs is initialized according to Glorot and Bengio (2010), who proposed this initialization scheme to bring substantially faster convergence. The weight matrix used for the linear transformation of the recurrent state is initialized as a random orthonormal matrix (Saxe et al., 2013; Mishkin and Matas, 2015) and the biases are initialized with zeros. Parameters are searched with RMSProp (learning rate 0.001) and mini-batches of size 128 over 1,000 epochs.

Results. Table 1 displays our main results in the two experiment settings, with WSCL and WSCR as testing data. Surprisingly, when we test the SOTA system of Peng et al. (2015a) on the *strict* WSCL data, the model fails to generalize. Again considering only the examples where the mention detection detected both and only both candidates and the pronoun was linked to one of them, it makes 24 correct and 22 false predictions and does not significantly outperform the random baseline (p=0.44). Our model experiences the same problem when trained on WSCR and tested on WSCL – a random process produces more or the same amount of correct predictions with p=0.14. The InferSent model, being pre-trained on large-scale NLI tasks proved to be a strong baseline and outperformed the baseline on both datasets by a notable margin, achieving the best result on WSCL (0.56 accuracy, significant on level p<0.05, non-significant for p<0.005). When trained on the WSCR training data and tested on the WSCR testing data, however our neural model significantly outperforms the random baseline by an observable margin of 9 percentage points (pp.) for Siam and 13 pp. for SiamE. A traditional coreference system and winner of the Conll 2011 Shared Task (Pradhan et al., 2011) is significantly outperformed by our neural model by 10 pp.

---

[8]http://cogcomp.cs.illinois.edu/page/software/_view/Winocoref
[9]Personal communication.
[10]https://github.com/facebookresearch/InferSent

Test	Siam		SiamE		Naïve		NaïveE		random		InferSent		SOTA	
	acc	p	acc	p	acc	p	acc	p	acc	p	acc	p	acc	p
WSCR	$0.59^{\pm0.02}$	0.00	**0.63**	0.00	$0.53^{\pm0.02}$	0.07	0.54	0.04	0.50	0.50	0.58	0.00	**0.76**[*]	0.00
WSCL	$0.51^{\pm0.01}$	0.30	0.54	0.13	$0.49^{\pm0.01}$	0.50	0.51	0.38	0.50	0.50	**0.56**	0.02	0.52[*]	0.44

Table 1: Test results for different systems on two WSC data sets. ⋆ means that the score is taken from Peng et al. (2015a) (for WSCR) or was approximated by applying the published tool as described in the text (for WSCL). Underlined p-values are smaller than 0.005. Averages and standard deviations are computed over five different random initializations of Siam (and Naïve), where we averaged over those five parameterizations that performed best on the development data. p-values for Siam and Naïve are computed using the predictions of the median accuracy model determined on the development set from the the five different random initializations. All neural models use data where noun phrase candidates are anonymized.

active feature	accuracy Siam	accuracy SiamE	
word sequence only	$0.57^{\pm0.02}$	0.59	
+ edges	$0.58^{\pm0.01}$	0.61	sequence level
+ connotation frames	$0.58^{\pm0.02}$	0.60	
- connotation frames	$0.59^{\pm0.02}$	0.60	
- edges	$0.59^{\pm0.01}$	0.61	
+ ConceptNet embedding	$0.59^{\pm0.01}$	0.61	NP level
- ConceptNet embedding	$0.58^{\pm0.01}$	0.59	
all active	$0.59^{\pm0.01}$	**0.63**	

Figure 4: Feature ablation experiments, where we are separately adding one of the different features to the word sequence input (+) or remove one feature from the model(-).

in accuracy when considering the ensemble model, and 6 pp. when considering the average of all five initializations with best scores on the development set (accuracy for the shared task winner was taken from (Rahman and Ng, 2012)). The naïve models fail to significantly outperform the random process strongly indicating that the Siamese ranking model is more suitable for the WSC task as it is optimized by directly learning the differences in interpretation among two highly similar proposed resolutions, one correct and one incorrect or implausible.

Anonymization. When we train and test our system on data which was *not* anonymized, the score of the Siamese ensemble model without features drops to 0.53 (p=0.059). The training loss decreased rapidly and the model exhibited little generalization capacity on unseen data. This indicates that – while neural models appear to have the potential to learn very abstract information needed for solving WSC from few data examples (561 twin pair training examples) – (i) they are very prone to overfitting when training data is scarce and not anonymized (it instantly remembers the surface noun phrases) and consequently (ii) anonymizing NPs can be very valuable for solving WSC problems, especially in a neural network setting. This is confirmed by our experiments with the neural InferSent, where the testing scores for anonymized data vs. non-anonymized data also differ observably (WSCR, non-anonymized: 0.52, anonymized: 0.58; WSCL, non-anonymized: 0.51, anonymized: 0.56).

Feature Ablations. To show the impact of individual features used in our feature-rich models Siam and SiamE, we perform experiments where we either (i) remove one specific feature from the model ('-' in Table 4) or (ii) add a single feature on top of the encoded sentence representation ('+' in Table 4). The results provide no clear picture but suggest that the complex features brought only small performance gains when applied individually, however, when applied jointly, they increase the model's performance observably from 0.59 to 0.63 accuracy. The ConceptNet NP phrase candidate level feature yields a performance increase of 2 pp. accuracy over the basic model and caused the largest drop of -4 pp. accuracy when removed from the model. On the positive side, our results suggest that non-linear neural models can learn abstract patterns based on word sequences *alone*, in contrast to successful methods from prior literature which all rely on linguistic annotation (e.g. dependency parsing) and carefully designed features and rules for accessing external knowledge bases. The Siamese model, trained *solely* on word sequences outperforms the random process significantly (p< 0.005).

Bill punched *Bob* in the face because **he** was being rude to Mary.
Bill punched Bob in the face because **he** wanted to protect Mary.
John introduced Bill because **he** knew everyone.
John introduced *Bill* because **he** was new.
John visited *Luke* in the hospital because **he** was sick.
John visited Luke in the hospital because **he** lived close by.

The boss fired *the worker* when **he** stopped performing well.
The boss fired the worker when **he** called him into the office.
The U.S.S Enterprise tried to assist a sister ship, but **they** arrived too late to save them.
The U.S.S Enterprise tried to assist *a sister ship*, but **they** did not receive help quick enough to prevent their demise.
Adam failed to kill *Alexander*, so **he** hired a bodygaurd in case of a second attempt.
Adam failed to kill Alexander, so **he** hired an assassin for the second attempt.

Figure 5: First box: Fully correctly resolved twin pair problems by all randomly initialized models. Second box: Fully falsely resolved twin pair problems by all randomly initialized models.

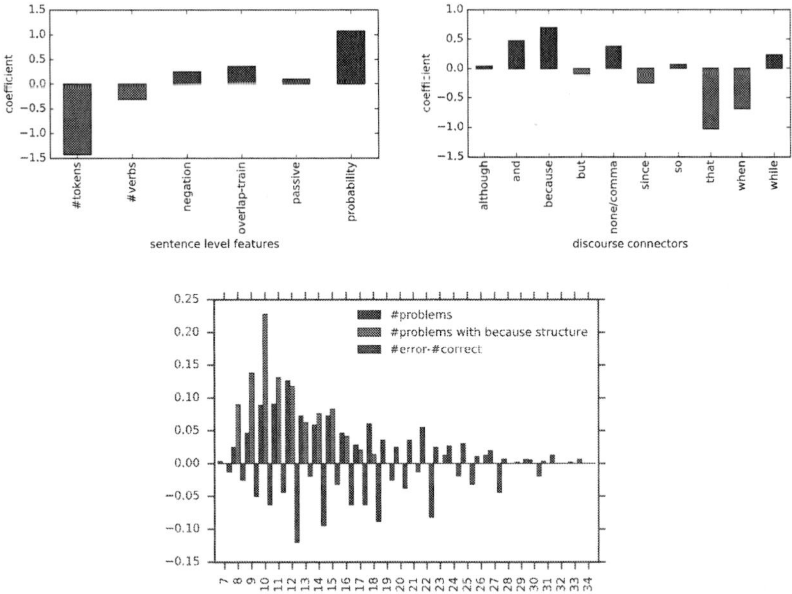

Figure 6: Coefficients for correct Siamese model guesses, sentence complexity features (left), discourse relations and *that*-conjunction (right). Bottom: Normalized distributions over sentence lengths: total (blue), problems with because-structure, amount of errors minus correct predictions. All statistics are computed from WSCR.

Deeper Analysis. In order to obtain deeper insight into the strengths and weaknesses of our model, we examine what properties discriminate the examples that our model solves successfully from the ones that it predicts erroneously. According to Levesque et al. (2012), it is critical to find a pair of twins that differ in one critical word in order to construct a full fledged WS, so it is natural that one may be interested in the model's performance over the twin pairs, i.e. the performance with respect to complete Winograd Schemata. Thereby we may also gain a better intuition of how vulnerable the model is with regard to changing the critical word. Figure 5 displays twin sentences from WSCR, where all five randomly initialized models came to the made the same prediction over the whole pair. Complete twin pairs were resolved correctly in 10 cases and incorrectly in 7 cases. The first case can be seen as 'most easy' for the model while we can conclude that the second case appeared to be the 'most difficult' or 'confusing' cases for the model. The examples suggest that the models perform better on sentences with unambiguous causal discourse markers (*because*) and less linguistic complexity (less verbs, shorter in length). To investigate more closely to what extent a successful resolution is informed by linguistic complexity, we designed 6 linguistic sentence-level features (length, number of verbs, passive construction, negation, sequence probability estimated with a language model and ratio of tokens to be found in the training data) and 10 binary features for different discourse connectors (*because, when, while*, etc.) and the sentence embedding conjunction *that*. From all five Siamese model initializations we collect the predictions, normalize the features onto a range between 0 and 1 and fit a regularized logistic regression model to predict a correct or incorrect prediction based on the aforementioned features. The coefficients of the features are displayed in Figure 6. The sequence length is strongly negatively correlated with a successful model prediction. On the other hand, the higher the estimated sentence probability and overlap with the training data, the more likely the Siamese model is to make a correct prediction. Perhaps more interesting are the coefficients for the discourse relation features. As the examples in (Figure 5) already suggested, the Siamese model performs better with the unambiguous causal discourse connector *because* as opposed to the ambiguous connector *when* or the sentence embedding conjunction *that*. However, this can also be explained by the fact that *because* is the most common discourse marker in the training data (698 occurrences in 1322 problems). Also, we found that problems involving *because* are generally shorter than other sentences in the data (see Figure 6, bottom).

6 Conclusion

Our assumption is that for interpreting Winograd sentences, humans process and build up a representation for full sentences, and that based on their understanding of the sentence with one or the other way of resolving the pronominal reference, they are able to decide which reading is correct. How exactly this is performed in terms of cognitive processes we cannot answer. However, the approach we are proposing offers two important ingredients of such a potential/hypothesized interpretation process: we formalized the WSC as a general sequence ranking problem and designed a Siamese neural network model that (i) computes full-fledged sentence interpretations as they would emerge from from resolving the pronominal anaphor to one or the other antecedent , and (ii) a ranking function that decides which of these interpretations can be assigned a higher confidence. Our Siamese model is able to solve a considerable amount of WSC challenge questions, after training it on pairs of sentence representations with correctly vs. incorrectly resolved anaphoric pronouns, where it learns information (features) that distinguishes these pairs. When applying the learned model to unseen pairs, it significantly outperforms not only a random process but also a naïve baseline neural model. While the model still lags behind state-of-the-art linear systems that rely on syntactic preprocessing and complex external knowledge sources accessed by manually designed features, our results are most promising: the Siamese sequence ranking model is able to learn how to resolve WS by only considering word sequences as input, and does so significantly better than the random baseline.

Cross-dataset experiments however showed that the WSC is far from being solved – while a state-of-the-art method and our system successfully answer many problems in one testing set (where the training data stems from the same source, created by a class of undergraduate students), *both* fail to generalize when presented a different, smaller WSC data set (where the examples perhaps are more carefully designed and seem notably more natural). On the smaller data both systems do not significantly outperform a random process. Because of this drastic drop in all of the model's performances and the small amounts of data we suggest that future work on the WSC should carefully test the methods on as much data as is available.

Our task formulation provides an easily accessible way for other researchers working on textual understanding to quickly test their sentence models on a very important AI and text understanding task.

Acknowledgements

This work has been supported by the German Research Foundation as part of the Research Training Group Adaptive Preparation of Information from Heterogeneous Sources (AIPHES) under grant No. GRK 1994/1 and by the Leibniz ScienceCampus "Empirical Linguistics and Computational Language Modeling", supported by the Leibniz Association grant no. SAS-2015-IDS-LWC and by the Ministry of Science, Research, and Art of Baden-Württemberg.

References

Collin F. Baker, Charles J. Fillmore, and John B. Lowe. 1998. The Berkeley FrameNet Project. In *Proceedings of the 36th Annual Meeting of the Association for Computational Linguistics and 17th International Conference on Computational Linguistics - Volume 1*, ACL '98, pages 86–90, Stroudsburg, PA, USA. Association for Computational Linguistics.

Chitta Baral. 2003. *Knowledge Representation, Reasoning, and Declarative Problem Solving*. Cambridge University Press, New York, NY, USA.

Samuel R. Bowman, Gabor Angeli, Christopher Potts, and Christopher D. Manning. 2015. A large annotated corpus for learning natural language inference. In *Proceedings of the 2015 Conference on Empirical Methods in Natural Language Processing (EMNLP)*. Association for Computational Linguistics.

Thorsten Brants and Alex Franz, 2006. *Web 1T 5-gram Version 1. Linguistic Data Consortium, Philadelphia, PA*. Philadelphia, PA.

Nathanael Chambers and Dan Jurafsky. 2008. Unsupervised learning of narrative event chains. In *Proceedings of ACL-08: HLT*, pages 789–797, Columbus, Ohio, June. Association for Computational Linguistics.

Alexis Conneau, Douwe Kiela, Holger Schwenk, Loïc Barrault, and Antoine Bordes. 2017. Supervised Learning of Universal Sentence Representations from Natural Language Inference Data. *CoRR*, abs/1705.02364.

Michael Gelfond and Vladimir Lifschitz. 1988. The Stable Model Semantics For Logic Programming. pages 1070–1080. MIT Press.

Xavier Glorot and Yoshua Bengio. 2010. Understanding the difficulty of training deep feedforward neural networks. In *In Proceedings of the International Conference on Artificial Intelligence and Statistics (AISTATS10). Society for Artificial Intelligence and Statistics*.

Sepp Hochreiter and Jürgen Schmidhuber. 1997. Long Short-Term Memory. *Neural Comput.*, 9(8):1735–1780, November.

Günter Klambauer, Thomas Unterthiner, Andreas Mayr, and Sepp Hochreiter. 2017. Self-Normalizing Neural Networks. *CoRR*, abs/1706.02515.

Canasai Kruengkrai, Naoya Inoue, Jun Sugiura, and Kentaro Inui. 2014. An Example-Based Approach to Difficult Pronoun Resolution. In *Proceedings of the 28th Pacific Asia Conference on Language, Information, and Computation*, pages 358–367, Phuket,Thailand, December. Department of Linguistics, Chulalongkorn University.

Heeyoung Lee, Yves Peirsman, Angel Chang, Nathanael Chambers, Mihai Surdeanu, and Dan Jurafsky. Stanford's Multi-pass Sieve Coreference Resolution System at the CoNLL-2011 Shared Task. In *Proceedings of the Fifteenth Conference on Computational Natural Language Learning: Shared Task*.

Kenton Lee, Luheng He, Mike Lewis, and Luke Zettlemoyer. 2017. End-to-end Neural Coreference Resolution. *CoRR*, abs/1707.07045.

Hector J. Levesque, Ernest Davis, and Leora Morgenstern. 2012. The Winograd Schema Challenge. In Gerhard Brewka, Thomas Eiter, and Sheila A. McIlraith, editors, *Principles of Knowledge Representation and Reasoning: Proceedings of the Thirteenth International Conference, KR 2012, Rome, Italy, June 10-14, 2012*. AAAI Press.

Hector J. Levesque. 2014. On our best behaviour. *Artificial Intelligence*, 212:27 – 35.

George A. Miller. 1995. WordNet: A Lexical Database for English. *Commun. ACM*, 38(11):39–41, November.

Dmytro Mishkin and Jiri Matas. 2015. All you need is a good init. *CoRR*, abs/1511.06422.

Haoruo Peng, Kai-Wei Chang, and Dan Roth. 2015a. A Joint Framework for Coreference Resolution and Mention Head Detection. In *CoNLL*, page 10, University of Illinois, Urbana-Champaign, Urbana, IL, 61801, 7. ACL.

Haoruo Peng, Daniel Khashabi, and Dan Roth. 2015b. Solving Hard Coreference Problems. In Rada Mihalcea, Joyce Yue Chai, and Anoop Sarkar, editors, *NAACL HLT 2015, The 2015 Conference of the North American Chapter of the Association for Computational Linguistics: Human Language Technologies, Denver, Colorado, USA, May 31 - June 5, 2015*, pages 809–819. The Association for Computational Linguistics.

Jeffrey Pennington, Richard Socher, and Christopher D. Manning. 2014. GloVe: Global Vectors for Word Representation. In *Empirical Methods in Natural Language Processing (EMNLP)*, pages 1532–1543.

Sameer Pradhan, Lance Ramshaw, Mitchell Marcus, Martha Palmer, Ralph Weischedel, and Nianwen Xue. 2011. CoNLL-2011 Shared Task: Modeling Unrestricted Coreference in OntoNotes. In *Proceedings of the Fifteenth Conference on Computational Natural Language Learning: Shared Task*, CONLL Shared Task '11, pages 1–27, Stroudsburg, PA, USA. Association for Computational Linguistics.

Altaf Rahman and Vincent Ng. 2012. Resolving Complex Cases of Definite Pronouns: The Winograd Schema Challenge. In *Proceedings of the 2012 Joint Conference on Empirical Methods in Natural Language Processing and Computational Natural Language Learning*, pages 777–789.

Hannah Rashkin, Sameer Singh, and Yejin Choi. 2015. Connotation Frames: Typed Relations of Implied Sentiment in Predicate-Argument Structure. *CoRR*, abs/1506.02739.

Hannah Rashkin, Sameer Singh, and Yejin Choi. 2016. Connotation Frames: A Data-Driven Investigation. In *Proceedings of the 54th Annual Meeting of the Association for Computational Linguistics, ACL 2016, August 7-12, 2016, Berlin, Germany, Volume 1: Long Papers*. The Association for Computer Linguistics.

Andrew M. Saxe, James L. McClelland, and Surya Ganguli. 2013. Exact solutions to the nonlinear dynamics of learning in deep linear neural networks. *CoRR*, abs/1312.6120.

Alexander Schrijver. 1986. *Theory of Linear and Integer Programming*. John Wiley & Sons, Inc., New York, NY, USA.

Peter Schüller. 2014. Tackling Winograd Schemas by Formalizing Relevance Theory in Knowledge Graphs. In *KR*. AAAI Press.

Arpit Sharma, Nguyen Ha Vo, Somak Aditya, and Chitta Baral. 2015. Towards Addressing the Winograd Schema Challenge - Building and Using a Semantic Parser and a Knowledge Hunting Module. In *IJCAI*, pages 1319–1325. AAAI Press.

Robert Speer and Catherine Havasi. 2012. Representing General Relational Knowledge in ConceptNet 5.

Robert Speer and Joanna Lowry-Duda. 2017. ConceptNet at SemEval-2017 Task 2: Extending Word Embeddings with Multilingual Relational Knowledge. *CoRR*, abs/1704.03560.

Finite State Reasoning for Presupposition Satisfaction

Jacob Collard
Cornell University
`jnc76@cornell.edu`

Abstract

Sentences with presuppositions are often treated as uninterpretable or unvalued (neither true nor false) if their presuppositions are not satisfied. However, there is an open question as to how this satisfaction is calculated. In some cases, determining whether a presupposition is satisfied is not a trivial task (or even a decidable one), yet native speakers are able to quickly and confidently identify instances of presupposition failure. I propose that this can be accounted for with a form of possible world semantics that encapsulates some reasoning abilities, but is limited in its computational power, thus circumventing the need to solve computationally difficult problems. This can be modeled using a variant of the framework of finite state semantics proposed by Rooth (2017). A few modifications to this system are necessary, including its extension into a three-valued logic to account for presupposition. Within this framework, the logic necessary to calculate presupposition satisfaction is readily available, but there is no risk of needing exceptional computational power. This correctly predicts that certain presuppositions will not be calculated intuitively, while others can be easily evaluated.

1 Introduction

Accounts of presupposition are typically concerned with describing the contexts in which a presupposition is satisfied, and with the syntactic and compositional factors which relate to the projection properties of presuppositions. However, there are a number of issues that can arise using the highly general methods for calculating presupposition satisfaction preferred by these accounts. Though many previous accounts roughly outline the sets in which a presupposition may be satisfied, they are not restrictive enough to allow for an actual computational implementation or to explain the cognitive reality of presupposition satisfaction.

Early work characterized presuppositions as relations between sentences and logical forms where a sentence A and a logical form L would be related iff A could only be uttered in contexts where L was entailed (Karttunen, 1973). Karttunen suggested a notion of presupposition satisfaction based on entailment, claiming that a context would satisfy the presuppositions of a sentence just in case the context entailed all of the basic presuppositions of the sentence. However, Karttunen does not explicitly define how the logical forms entailed by a context are calculated. Instead, he simply defines the context as "a set of logical forms that describe the set of background assumptions, that is, whatever the speaker chooses to regard as being shared by him and his intended audience." How a speaker determines this set of logical forms notwithstanding, it is not trivial to calculate the set of logical forms entailed by another.

Advances since Karttunen (1973) have focused on capturing the appropriate empircal details of presupposition projection. However, the basic notion of presupposition as a relation between sentences and logical forms depending on context remains unchanged. Other ideas still in common circulation today are even older, dating back to Frege (1892). One important such idea is the notion that sentences with presuppositions can carry any one of three possible true values: T(rue), F(alse), or (N)either, though

Proceedings of the First International Workshop on Language Cognition and Computational Models, pages 53–62
Santa Fe, New Mexico, United States, August 20, 2018.
https://doi.org/10.18653/v1/P17

this precise naming convention follows Belnap (1979). Such notions remain important through accounts such as the partial account proposed by Beaver and Krahmer (2001).

Beaver and Krahmer's account diverges somewhat from Karttunen's in that it is, in some sense, less pragmatic in that it accounts for presuppositions in the truth conditions of each sentence. For the interface between semantics and pragmatics, Beaver & Krahmer rely only on a valuation function $V : \mathbb{P} \to T, F$, which maps atomic propositions to truth values. Notably, this function's range does not include N, as atomic propositions never carry their own presuppositions. Instead, the determination of presupposition failure falls to the logical form of the sentence and the logical operators on these truth values. As an example, the sentence in (1) could be represented with the logical form in (2), where p represents the proposition "Mary is sad" and q represents the proposition that Bill regrets that Mary is sad (without its presupposition).

(1) Bill regrets that Mary is sad.

(2) $(\partial p \wedge q) \vee \neg \partial p$

For valuations where $V(p) = F$, this formula will evaluate to N, while in valuations where $V(p) = T$ it will evaluate to T or F, depending on the value of $V(q)$. However, once again, this is more complicated in practice than it seems. Actually representing V explicitly in complex situations could require solving some very difficult computational problems. Defining V for all possible propositions is not feasible in a computational environment (including the human brain) unless many values can be predicted from others. However, this amounts to the same problem that I mentioned for Karttunen's model: calculating the set of propositions entailed by another set.

In this paper, I consider this problem more formally, and tackle it by means of a somewhat more restrictive semantics that is incapable of representing complex computational problems, but nonetheless is able to capture the "core" semantics of most concepts. The kinds of reasoning that are necessary for natural language phenomena – in this case, presupposition satisfaction – are within the realm of possibility for this formalism, but more difficult problems never arise. In §2, I further specify the problem of difficult entailment calculations for presupposition. In §3, I re-introduce the formalism of finite state semantics, following work by Rooth (2017). I expand upon this work in §4, introducing finite state semantics for presupposition. Lastly, I discuss the formalism's strengths and weaknesses, consider other possible explanations, and conclude in §5.

A sample implementation of the concepts presented in this paper is available at `https://github.com/thorsonlinguistics/finite-state-presupposition`.

2   Difficult Entailment Problems

Before I consider the general problem of explicit presupposition satisfaction, it may be helpful to consider a few examples where calculating presupposition satisfaction is difficult.

In some contexts, calculating presupposition satisfaction is not possible at all. A simple example occurs with nonce forms and factive verbs, as in (3).

(3) Sam knows that Taylor is a garchank.

Without knowing what a garchank is, an interlocutor cannot determine whether Taylor is one, and thus cannot calculate whether the presupposition is true. However, the interlocutors clearly still have intuitions about the presuppositions of this sentence and it is even possible to construct contexts where the presupposition is clearly satisfied, or where it is clearly *not* satisfied, as in (4) and (5), respectively.

(4) Taylor is a garchank and Sam knows that Taylor is a garchank.

(5) Taylor is not a garchank, but Sam knows that Taylor is a garchank.

Without additional accommodation, (5) is intuitively infelicitous in all contexts, as the factive presupposition that Taylor is a garchank is explicitly contradicted. However, what about (6)? Without knowing what both garchank and quiblet mean, it is again impossible to determine whether the presupposition is satisfied.

(6)   Taylor is a quiblet and Sam knows that Taylor is a garchank.

Crucially, presupposition satisfaction is not always *syntactic* (in the logical sense). That is, the fact that *Taylor is not a garchank* ($\neg g$) contradicts *Taylor is a garchank* (g) can be easily determined by the syntactic formulation of the corresponding logical formulas – it is syntactically derivable that any pair of formulas of the form p and $\neg p$ will be contradictory. However, it is *not* syntactically derivable that q and g are contradictory, where q means "Taylor is a quiblet" and g means "Taylor is a garchank." Without further axiomatization to specify that $q \rightarrow \neg g$, the presupposition satisfaction cannot be derived, though speakers still have some intuitions about what it might take for the sentence to be felicitous. When this axiom is introduced, however, it becomes possible to determine that (6) is, in fact, infelicitous.

Consider a more concrete example. Since most native speakers of English know that birds are not mammals, it is fairly intuitive to determine that (8) is an infelicitous utterance in most contexts. However, as described above, this requires knowledge of certain axioms implied by the lexical entries or by the speaker's world knowledge.

(7)   Taylor is a cat and Sam knows that Taylor is an mammal.

(8)   Taylor is a bird and Sam knows that Taylor is a mammal.

In most cases, this is not actually a problem: the interlocutors are aware of these axioms and can calculate whether they are true in context, whether they are entailed by the linguistic environment, or whether they just aren't known yet (as is the case in (6) without additional information about the meaning of garchank and quiblet).

However, in other cases, it will, in fact *never* be possible to accurately determine whether the presupposition is satisfied. (9), for example, makes reference to the halting problem, which specifies that it is *undecidable* whether an arbitrary program will halt for all possible inputs.

(9)   Sam knows that every program on the computer halts.

Can an interlocutor determine whether the presupposition in (9) is satisfied in context? In some contexts, yes. Some programs, of course, do halt, and it may be that all of the programs on the computer do. However, in other contexts, the interlocutors will not be able to determine this fact. Again, the interlocutors still know the conditions under which the sentence is felicitous, but they cannot evaluate this with respect to all possible contexts.

If additional information is added to the scenario, interlocutors may be able to perform additional reasoning. For example, the interlocutors may know that all of the programs on the computer contain 'while' loops that never exit, effectively meaning that none of the programs halt and thus that the presupposition is not satisfied. However, for an arbitrary set of programs, even if that set is fully specified, they cannot determine the felicity of (9).

This poses an important problem. If speakers of natural language perform entailment reasoning in *some* presuppositional contexts, such as (8), but not in others, such as (9), then there is an open question of exactly which sentences fall under which category. Furthermore, since presupposition satisfaction seems to be, in cases like (8), a fairly intuitive, linguistic process, it seems probable that presupposition satisfaction in these cases needs to be calculated fairly quickly. This poses additional problems for cases where presupposition satisfaction *can* be calculated, but requires significant computation.

As an example of a presupposition that is possible, but difficult, to calculate, consider a scenario where the speaker is discussing a checkers game between Sam and Taylor. The speaker may utter the sentence in (10). Actually calculating whether Taylor did make the optimal move in any given situation is possible, but could be quite difficult (Fraenkel et al., 1978). Adding additional discourse information could indicate that Taylor did *not* make the correct move, but the intuition remains that the presupposition might be satisfied – interlocutors do not necessarily know intuitively whether (11) is felicitous.

(10)   Taylor knows that she made the optimal move.

(11)   Taylor did not queen her piece when she could have, but she knows that she made the optimal move.

In other words, humans only calculate presupposition satisfaction when it is easy. This computation may become easy under various different circumstances, such as when the presupposition is directly stated or once a hard calculation is completed (and accepted by all interlocutors and thus added to the common ground). However, some calculations are *always* easy, such as the contradictory case in (8). Such calculations can be factored into the semantics to account for the intuitive nature of these calculations. I hypothesize that these "easy" calculations are exactly those calculations which can be represented using finite state semantics. Finite state semantics will represent a set of possible worlds for each sentence and will capture the reasoning necessary to capture presupposition satisfaction in some cases, but not in others. In cases where presupposition satisfaction cannot be directly calculated by finite state semantics, the conditions can still be represented and satisfaction can still be characterized.

3   Finite State Semantics

Finite state semantics of the sort that I will utilize here was proposed by Rooth (2017) and itself makes use of the finite state calculus developed by Morhi and Sproat (1996) and Kempe and Karttunen (1996). An implementation of the finite state calculus that could be used for representing finite state semantics is FOMA (Hulden, 2006), which allows for the creation of finite state machines and finite state transducers based on extended regular expressions.

Finite state semantics represents each sentence as a formula of finite state calculus, which can be compiled into a finite state machine (or, in some cases, a finite state transducer). This represents either the set of worlds in which the sentence is true or a relation between worlds (as in the case of questions, following Groenendijk and Stokhof (2002)). I will focus on the case of declarative sentences.

Finite state semantics relies heavily on the notion of centering (Bittner, 2003). As finite state machines are generally capable only of representing sets of strings or binary relations on strings, centering is necessary to distinguish individuals to allow for reference. As an example, the lexical entry for a word such as "cat" would describe the set of worlds in which the center (the most distinguished individual) was a cat. This is done by representing the world as a sequence of individuals, where each individual is defined by a number of properties, including whether the agent has observed it, whether it is the center (or the secondary center, also called the pericenter), and any other characteristics it may have (such as being a cat).

The following definitions show how individuals might be constructed in a model of finite state semantics. There are four kinds of distinguished individuals, represented by the set IDX. These are traces, centers, pericenters, and null, represented by I_0, I_1, I_2, and $I_\varnothing$, respectively. Centers and pericenters are distinguished individuals, with pericenters being secondary (the existence of a pericenter always implies the existence of a center). Null centers are not distinguished and are the default for individuals. Traces are not used in this paper, but are important for the representation of relative clauses. The machine represented by ID is the set of the possible identifiers for elements, which in this case are simple descriptions of the kind of individual being referenced, such as a cat or a dog. In more complex models, these may be much richer representations.

Definition 1 INDIVIDUAL := KNO ID IDX

Definition 2 KNO := $K^+ \cup K^-$

Definition 3 ID := CAT $\cup$ DOG $\ldots$

Definition 4 IDX := $I_0 \cup I_1 \cup I_2 \cup I_\varnothing$

Instances of individuals can be strung together geometrically to create grid-like worlds. For simplicity, I will use only a one-dimensional world, which consists primarily of a string of individuals. The set of all possible worlds is referred to as W. Each proposition is a subset of W indicating the worlds where the proposition is true.

As an example, a simple sentence such as (12) can be translated into finite state semantics using the formula (13). This formula is comparable to the predicate logic formula (14), except that functions such as HASID and INDEF can be reduced to formulas operating directly on finite state machines. The primitive finite state machines in this example include the set of all possible worlds W, as well as worlds in which the center has the symbol CAT, worlds where the center has the symbol DOG, and worlds where the center is adjacent to the pericenter.

(12)   A cat is adjacent to a dog.

(13) $\text{INDEF}(\text{HASID}(\text{CAT}), \text{INDEF}(\text{HASID}(\text{DOG}), \text{ADJ}))$

(14) $\exists x[\text{CAT}(x) \wedge \exists y[\text{DOG}(y) \wedge \text{ADJ}(x,y)]]$

Each expression on (13) evaluates to a particular proposition, most of which are intersected together to produce the final proposition, though some additional operations are necessary. For example, the expression $\text{HASID}(\text{DOG})$ indicates the set of worlds in W where the center has the identifier DOG. The expression ADJ represents the set of worlds where the center is adjacent to the pericenter. When ADJ and DOG are intersected, they represent the set of worlds where the center is a dog and is adjacent to the pericenter. The expression $\text{INDEF}(\text{HASID}(\text{DOG}, \text{ADJ}))$ further operates on this set to produce the set of worlds where the center is adjacent to a dog (by promoting the pericenter to the center and removing the center). Ultimately, the formula in (13) represents the set of worlds where an individual with the identifier CAT is adjacent to an individual with the identifier DOG.

Of course, it is possible to define much more complex expressions in order to represent other sentences of natural language. In particular, Rooth (2017) defines mechanics for representing intensional semantics and questions using finite state transducers. Rooth also describes how formulas might be produced compositionally from lexical entries using categorial grammars. Crucially, however, finite state semantics provides a compositional means of explicitly representing the set of worlds in which a proposition is true. Reasoning can be introduced by restricting the set using axioms, and some reasoning can even be earned "for free" from the structure of the set of worlds (for example, in this one-dimensional model, it is only possible for an individual to be adjacent to two other individuals).

There is some reasoning, however, that finite state semantics cannot do. For example, attempting to represent sentences such as (15) is difficult. Because the set of worlds where the number of cats and dogs are equal is not a regular set, it cannot be represented using a finite state machine. However, it is still possible to represent, generally speaking, the conditions on the set of worlds. Though Rooth does not discuss this, additional propositions can be easily affixed to the description of each world.

(15)   There are the same number of cats as dogs.

Note that no matter the level of computation used, this sort of technique will be necessary for some sentences, such as (9), above. The precise set of worlds where every program halts cannot be fully described by the semantics, so it is necessary to simply state the condition, without fully restricting the set. Note that this will always produce a set of worlds that is *larger* than the "actual" set. As such, this isn't necessarily a problem, it simply indicates a clear boundary between computations that can be carried out in the semantics, and computations that cannot. If finite state semantics is an accurate model of human reasoning, than only finite state computations are performed in the semantics, while other computations are left to higher-level reasoning systems.

However, Rooth's finite state semantics does not provide any mechanism for dealing with presuppositions.

4   Finite State Semantics for Presuppositions

In order to account for presuppositions, I mostly follow Beaver and Krahmer (2001) and use a three-valued logic with Strong Kleene operations. Beaver and Krahmer account for presupposition using a unary presupposition operator ∂ and a binary operator called transplication. The unary presupposition operator has the following truth table.

The transplication operator used by Beaver and Krahmer can be defined using the Strong Kleene connectives $\wedge$, $\vee$, and $\neg$ as well as the partial operator above, such that $\varphi_{\langle \pi \rangle}$ (the proposition φ with the presupposition π) is equivalent to $(\partial \pi \wedge \varphi) \vee \neg \partial \pi$.

As such, there are only a few tasks that need to be undertaken in order to convert Rooth's finite state semantics into finite state semantics with presupposition. First, the basic model needs to be refined in

x	∂ x
T	T
F	N
N	N

Table 1: Unary presupposition

order to account for three-valued logic. Second, the Strong Kleene connectives and the partial operator need to be defined. Finally, these components need to be put together to produce the transplication operator.

The previous model of finite state semantics was incapable of representing three-valued logic because every world in the set was "true", while the set's complement was "false". I account for three-valued logic simply by specifying that every defined world appears in the set and is annotated as either true or false. This produces a set of *valued* worlds W_V instead of a simple set of worlds.[1]

The set of valued worlds can be defined quite trivially from the set W, as shown in Definition 5. Each world in W is simply preceded by a symbol indicating whether it is true or false.

Definition 5 $W_V := (\text{TRUE} \cup \text{FALSE})\ W$

Defining the Strong Kleene connectives is somewhat less trivial, but can still be done. Strong Kleene "and" is true if both of its arguments are true, and false if either of its arguments are false. Similarly, Strong Kleene "or" is false if both of its arguments are false and true if either one is true. Otherwise, it is neither true nor false. With this in mind, the definitions below can be constructed, where W_t is the set of worlds annotated as "true" and W_f is the set of worlds annotated "false".

Definition 6 $\text{KAND}(X, Y) := W_V \cap ((W_t \cap X \cap Y) \cup (W_f \cap X) \cup (W_f \cap Y))$

Definition 7 $\text{KOR}(X, Y) := W_V \cap ((W_f \cap X \cap Y) \cup (W_t \cap X) \cup (W_t \cap Y))$

Strong Kleene negation can be constructed simply by transducing true worlds to false worlds and vice versa. In this definition, $\text{CO}(X)$ indicates the co-domain of a binary relation, while Σ indicates the set of all possible symbols in finite state semantics.

Definition 8 $\text{KNOT}(X) := W_V \cap \text{CO}(X \circ ((\text{TRUE} \times \text{FALSE}) \cup (\text{FALSE} \times \text{TRUE})\ \Sigma^*))$

Lastly, the partial operator can be defined as the set of valued worlds in W_V where false worlds are removed from the argument – only true worlds are valid.

Definition 9 $\text{PRESUPPOSITION}(X) := W_V \cap (X - W_F)$

Translating the transplication operator at this point is trivial, as all of the operators necessary have already been defined: Strong Kleene connectives and unary presupposition.

Definition 10 $\text{TRANSPLICATE}(X, Y) := \text{KOR}(\text{KAND}(\text{PRESUPPOSITION}(Y), X),$
$\text{KNOT}(\text{PRESUPPOSITION}(Y)))$

With this tool, it becomes possible to define many presuppositions using finite state semantics, including an extension of Rooth's (2017) intensional semantics for "know" to include a factive presupposition and definite descriptions with uniqueness or maximality presuppositions.

4.1 Factive Presuppositions

Factive presuppositions are introduced by verbs such as *know* in sentences such as (16). The presupposition is satisfied in contexts where the complement of the verb is true.

(16)   The agent knows that a cat is adjacent to a dog.

---

[1]In principle, this actually accounts for a four-valued logic, as there is nothing that prevents a world from being annotated both as a true world and as a false world. Getting rid of this generalization would make the definition of W_V slightly more complicated, and as such I have ignored this possibility. Four-valued logics have also been presented as in some ways "more natural" by, e.g., Herzberger (1973), Karttunen and Peters (1979), and Cooper (1983), which Beaver and Krahmer (2001) note as well.

Assuming that there exists some formula $K(X)$ which indicates that the agent has observed X to be true, it is straightforward to apply the transplication operator to create a factive presupposition, as in (17). For the purposes of this paper, I will only discuss single-agent systems; extending K to a two-place predicate and extending the model to account for multiple agents is left as a future exercise.

(17) TRANSPLICATE(K(X), X)

Rooth (2017) does provide an implementation for $K(X)$, though it requires some modification to work with presuppositions. In particular, the model needs to ensure that any presuppositions that X introduces on its own are projected into the matrix sentence. For example, consider example (18), which contains an embedded presupposition. This sentence is felicitous only where "the cat" can be uniquely identified *and* the cat is adjacent to a dog.

(18) The agent knows that the cat is adjacent to a dog.

Constructing this appropriate definition for $K(X)$ does require a fairly complex definition, but the intuition behind these definitions is simply that the undefined worlds of X are removed. Otherwise, the definition is mostly a straightforward translation of Kripke semantics. R was similarly defined in Rooth (2017); the basic notion behind this relation is that elements which have observed do not vary in the accessible worlds, while other elements are free to vary. This creates an epistemic accessibility relation. K_{base} is the true component of $K(X)$ and is separated from $K(X)$ only in the interest of clarity. UNDEFINEDWORLDS, FALSEWORLDS, and TRUEWORLDS are functions which extract the undefined, false-valued, and true-valued component of a set of valued worlds.

Definition 11 $R := \text{ID} \rightarrow \text{ID} \mid \text{K}^{-}\_$

Definition 12 $K_{base}(X) := \text{TRUE } (W - \text{DO}(R \circ \text{FALSEWORLDS}(X)))$

Definition 13 $K(X) := W_V \cap (K_{base}(X) \cup (\text{FALSE } (W - \text{DEFINEDWORLDS}(K_{base}(X))))) - \text{UNDEFINEDWORLDS}(X)$

These definitions produce the appropriate predictions about presuppositions and presupposition projection. The formula in (19) does not contain any worlds, either in its true or false component, that contain more than one cat or where the cat is not adjacent to the dog.

(19) $K(\text{DEF}(\text{HASID}(\text{CAT}), \text{INDEF}(\text{DOG}, \text{ADJ})))$

4.2 Maximality

As a second example, I consider the case of definite descriptions. The basic notion is, of course, the same: definite descriptions will introduce a formula of the form TRANSPLICATE(X, Y), where X is the main proposition introduced by the lexical entry and Y is its presupposition. In this case, the presupposition is some form of maximality, indicating that there is a unique collection of individuals that satisfy the restrictor. The other argument of transplication in this case will be a normal application of INDEF. Definites introduce very similar relations when compared to indefinites; they simply have an additional presupposition. The general definition of definites is given below.

Definition 14 $\text{DEF}(X, Y) := \text{TRANSPLICATE}(\text{INDEF}(X, Y), \text{UNIQUE}(X))$

There are, of course, a number of theories describing precisely how the presupposition for definites should be constructed (Elbourne, 2013). Many of these theories introduce a simple uniqueness constraint (Kadmon, 1990; Elbourne, 2008; Roberts, 2003). For illustrative purposes in this paper, I will consider only this simple constraint, which only works for singular definites. The implementation of plural definites is given in the supplementary code.

In this case, the intuition behind UNIQUE(X) is that there can only be one center that satisfies the property X. In worlds where the center currently satisfies X, but a *different* center in the same basic world could also satisfy X, UNIQUE(X) is not true. A similar intuition can be applied for maximality.

Describing uniqueness requires allowing worlds to (at least temporarily) contain multiple centers and/or multiple pericenters. Of course, this is necessary for describing plurals as well, and so it is not an unexpected complication. In addition, uniqueness requires the ability to arbitrarily re-assign centers. This is done with the DoReBind predicate.

Definition 15 $\text{ReBind} := (\text{Idx} \to \text{Idx}) \cap (W \times W)$

Definition 16 $\text{DoReBind}(X) := \text{Co}(X \circ \text{ReBind})$

Using DoReBind, it is again fairly straightforward to define the uniqueness presupposition. The Value predicate takes a set of worlds and produces the corresponding set of valued worlds. Again, the undefined worlds of X are removed in order to ensure that presuppositions project properly.

Definition 17 $\text{Unique}(X) := \text{Value}(\text{DoReBind}(\text{TrueWorlds}(X) - \text{DoReBind}(\text{TrueWorlds}(X) \cap (\Sigma^* I_1 \Sigma^* I_1 \Sigma^*)))), X) - \text{UndefinedWorlds}(X)$

This definition of Unique is used in Definition 14 to construct the lexical entry for the singular definite article. Any reasoning that can be handled by the finite state machine will be automatically calculated in determining the set of valued worlds.

5 Conclusion

By extending Rooth's (2017) finite state semantics to include presupposition, I have also shown how presupposition satisfaction might be calculated in an intelligent system. Crucially, the finite state semantics described here calculates presupposition satisfaction efficiently, without risk of coming across undecidable or computationally expensive problems. There remains some question as to whether finite state semantics is an accurate model of *human* reasoning with respect to presupposition satisfaction and the semantics-pragmatics interface, but it is a *possible* solution.

With this in mind, it is useful to consider the precise predictions that finite state semantics makes for future, empirical work on the psycholinguistics of presupposition satisfaction. Finite state semantics is capable of reasoning about any entailment patterns that are the result of relations between regular sets. Consider the simple, one-dimensional model used in the semantic formulas above. In this model, it is only possible for an element to be adjacent to two other elements. If sentences (20) and (21) are both true (and both refer to the same cat), then the cat cannot *also* be adjacent to a penguin, and the presupposition in (22) should fail according to finite state semantics.

(20)   The cat is adjacent to a dog.

(21)   The cat is adjacent to a rabbit.

(22)   The agent knows that the cat is adjacent to a penguin.

Intuitively, this seems to be true! In a more realistic environment, consider a movie theater, where patrons sit next to each other in a row. A patron can only be sitting next to, at most, two other people, as the people behind and in front of the patron are not usually considered "next to" the guest. Sentence (23) does not seem to be felicitous.

(23)   # Sam is sitting next to Taylor and Riley, but Dylan knows that Sam is sitting next to Logan.

On the other hand, there are some contexts that finite state semantics cannot capture. The examples in (9) and (10) are two such cases, for which humans clearly do not calculate the exact set of worlds where the presupposition is satisfied.

Still, there are some cases that are less clear. Finite state semantics is not capable of representing sets that are not regular, including anything higher in the Chomsky hierarchy: context-free languages, context-sensitive languages, or recursively enumerable languages. Constructing natural examples for these sets is difficult, especially as, for more restrictive models, finite state semantics is capable of representing sets that would not be regular in larger models. For example, the set of worlds where (24) is true is not regular. However, if the size of the world is bounded (i.e., no worlds above a particular size are represented in the model), then it can still be represented by finite state semantics.

(24)   There are an equal number of cats and dogs.

However, there is additional evidence against a context-free or recursively enumerable semantics, namely that context-free languages are not closed under intersection and recursively enumerable languages are not closed under complement, both of which are used extensively in semantics and reasoning about presuppositions. As such, having a context-free or recursively enumerable semantics as opposed to a regular one would not guarantee cohesion; in some cases, the system would need to rely on more computationally powerful system to represent the desired set at all. Finite state semantics is always capable of producing a set, even if that set is occasionally larger than necessary. Recursively enumerable semantics is especially problematic, as it would require super-Turing computation, thus violating the Church-Turing thesis.

As such, finite state semantics seems to be a reasonable candidate for natural language reasoning for presuppositions, and for many other semantic and pragmatic phenomena besides. Though other solutions to this problem may be possible, especially within the scope of context-sensitive semantics, which would have all of the necessary closure properties, it is generally desirable to make use of the weakest level of computational complexity required, as higher levels of computation are often less efficient. In particular, finite state semantics is capable of representing large sets of possible worlds and performing its calculations in reasonable amounts of time and space, while still representing enough of the semantics to reason about presupposition and provide an interface to higher-level reasoning.

Acknowledgements

Many thanks to the LCCM reviewers, Mats Rooth, Joseph Halpern, and John Foster for their comments.

References

David Beaver and Emiel Krahmer. 2001. A partial account of presupposition projection. *Journal of Logic, Language, and Information*, (10):147–182.

Nuel Belnap, 1979. *A useful four-valued logic*, pages 8–37. Reidel, Dordrecht.

Maria Bittner. 2003. Word order and incremental update. In *Annual Meeting of the Chicago Linguistic Society*, volume 39, pages 634–664. Chicago Linguistic Society.

Robin Cooper. 1983. *Quantification and Syntactic Theory*. Reidel, Dordrecht.

Paul Elbourne. 2008. Demonstratives as individual concepts. *Linguistics and Philosophy*, 31:409–466.

Paul Elbourne. 2013. *Definite Descriptions*. Oxford University Press, Oxford.

A. S. Fraenkel, M. R. Garey, D. S. Johnson, T. Schaefer, and Y. Yesha. 1978. The complexity of checkers on an $N \times N$ board. In *19th International Symposium on Foundations of Computer Science*, pages 55–64, October.

Gottlob Frege. 1892. Über sinn und bedeutung. *Zeitschrift für Philosophie und philosophische Kritik*, (100):25–50.

Jeroen Groenendijk and Martin Stokhof. 2002. Type-shifting rules and the semantics of interrogatives. In Paul Portner and Barbara H. Partee, editors, *Formal Semantics: The Essential Readings*, pages 421–456. Blackwell.

Hans Herzberger. 1973. Dimensions of truth. *Journal of Philosophical Logic*, (2):535–556.

Mans Hulden. 2006. Finite-state syllabification. In Anssi Yli-Jyrä, Lauri Karttunen, and Juhani Karhumäki, editors, *Finite-State Methods and Natural Language Processing*, volume 4002 of *Lecture Notes in Artificial Intelligence*. Springer.

Nirit Kadmon. 1990. Uniqueness. *Linguistics and Philosophy*, 13:173–324.

Lauri Karttunen and Stanley Peters. 1979. Conventional implicature. In C. Oh and D. Dinneen, editors, *Presupposition*, volume 11 of *Syntax and Semantics*, pages 1–56. Academic Press, New York.

Lauri Karttunen. 1973. Presupposition and linguistic context. *Theoretical Linguistics*, (1):181–194.

André Kempe and Lauri Karttunen. 1996. Parallel replacement in the finite-state calculus. In *Sixteenth International Conference on Computational Linguistics*.

Mehryar Morhi and Richard Sproat. 1996. An efficient compiler for weighted rewrite rules. In *34th Annual Meeting of the Association for Computational Linguistics*.

Craige Roberts. 2003. Uniqueness in definite noun phrases. *Linguistics and Philosophy*, 26:287–350.

Mats Rooth. 2017. Finite state intensional semantics. In *International Conference on Computational Semantics*, Montpellier, September.

Language-Based Automatic Assessment of Cognitive and Communicative Functions Related to Parkinson's Disease

Gabriel Murray
Computer Information Systems
U. of the Fraser Valley
Abbotsford, BC, Canada
`gabriel.murray@ufv.ca`

Lesley Jessiman
Psychology
U. of the Fraser Valley
Abbotsford, BC, Canada
`lesley.jessiman@ufv.ca`

McKenzie Braley
Psychology
U. of the Fraser Valley
Abbotsford, BC, Canada
`mckenzie.braley@student.ufv.ca`

Abstract

We explore the use of natural language processing and machine learning for detecting evidence of Parkinson's disease from transcribed speech of subjects who are describing everyday tasks. Experiments reveal the difficulty of treating this as a binary classification task, and a multi-class approach yields superior results. We also show that these models can be used to predict cognitive abilities across all subjects.

1 Introduction

Parkinson's disease (PD) is the second most prevalent neurodegenerative disease worldwide, affecting more than one percent of individuals above the age of 60 (deRijk et al., 2000; von Campenhausen et al., 2005). PD is associated with the gradual degeneration of dopaminergic neurons in the substantia nigra pars compacta in the basal ganglia (Bottcher, 1975; Samii et al., 2004). Dopamine depletion originating in the basal ganglia leads to an under-activation of the frontal lobes, where motor functions and executive processing are predominantly housed. Fronto-striate pathway disturbances lead to motor impairments such as resting tremors, muscular rigidity, bradykinesia and postural disturbances (Samii et al., 2004; von Campenhausen et al., 2005). Motor-related speech deficits are also observed. One of the most common speech problems is a marked decrease in the volume of the PD sufferer's voice, known as *aphonia* (Nutt et al., 1992). PD can also impair the individual's use of vocal parameters, preventing them from appropriately stressing and emphasizing particular words (Dubois, 1991). Short bursts of speech coupled with long pauses (Darley et al., 1975), accelerated speech (*tachiphemia*), compulsive repetition of words or phrases (*palilalia*) (Boller et al., 1975), and stuttering (Lebrun, 1996) are also observed in some individuals with PD. All of the aforementioned speech and language impairments stem from PD-related motor decline.

A gradual decline in dopaminergic neurons in the basal ganglia and a subsequent disturbance of the fronto-striate loop also leads to language impairments related to an executive processing dysfunction. The research shows that PD results in deficits in word-finding/verbal fluency (Gurd and Oliveira, 1996; Henry and Crawford, 2004; Matison et al., 1982; Randolph et al., 1993; Zec et al., 1999), syntactical processing (Arnott et al., 2005; Illes, 1989; Grossman et al., 1992; Grossman et al., 1996; Grossman et al., 2000; Hochstadt et al., 2006; Kemmerer, 1999; Kemmerer, 1999; Lieberman et al., 1992; Natsopoulos et al., 1991; Ullman et al., 1997), and speech error monitoring (McNamara et al., 1992). There is also evidence that PD individuals score lower on measures of pragmatic communication abilities such as conversational appropriateness, speech acts, stylistics, gestures and prosodics (McNamara and Durso, 2003).

Proceedings of the First International Workshop on Language Cognition and Computational Models, pages 63–74
Santa Fe, New Mexico, United States, August 20, 2018.
https://doi.org/10.18653/v1/P17

Many of the language deficits reported have been attributed to impaired working memory, namely executive function of working memory (Grossman et al., 1992; Grossman et al., 2000; Kemmerer, 1999). It is worth noting that one of the most well-documented problems in the PD and cognition literature is of course working memory decline (Dirnberger and Jahanshahi, 2013; Gabrieli et al., 1996; Lee et al., 2010). Other cognitive deficits associated with PD are set-shifting deficits (Gauntlett-Gilbert et al., 1999), poor Theory of Mind (Bora et al., 2015), and visual working memory impairments (Zhao et al., 2018).

Given that PD results in changes in the comprehension and production of language and also the awareness of one's own communicative ability, it would seem reasonable to assume that language could be used as a diagnostic tool and a means of monitoring the progression of PD. The aim of this work is thus to automatically detect evidence of PD by extracting linguistic features from textual transcripts generated by participants with PD. Although there is some research that has looked at the acoustic features of speech to detect PD, an examination of linguistic features from textual transcripts is a more neglected area. We first show that it is difficult to approach this as a binary classification task (i.e., with or without PD), particularly because of linguistic similarities between healthy older adults and older adults with PD. We subsequently show that better prediction performance can be had by treating automated detection as a multi-class classification problem. Specifically, we classify participants into one of three groups: healthy younger adults (HYA), healthy older adults (HOA), and older adults with PD (PD). Finally, we show that the same set of linguistic features can be used to predict cognitive performance scores across all subjects.

The structure of this paper is as follows. In Section 2, we discuss related work on using machine learning and speech and language processing to detect age-related conditions, as well as research on linguistic abilities and cognitive functions. In Section 3 we describe how the data in this study were collected, including the participant cohorts, the description tasks given to them, and the cognitive scores that were measured. In Section 4, we describe the linguistic features, machine learning models, and evaluation metrics used. Section 5 presents a series of experiments and key results. We conclude and discuss future work in Section 6.

2 Related Work

In the past few years, there has been an increase in research on the detection of aging pathologies using speech and language processing techniques. For example, using spoken language samples elicited in the clinical setting, Roark and colleagues (2011) were able to discriminate older adults with mild cognitive impairment (MCI) from those who showed no evidence of MCI. Masrani et al. (2017b) used domain adaptation techniques that exploit existing data resources from the source domain of Alzheimer's disease (AD) to improve detection in the target domain of MCI. Fraser, Meltzer and Rudzicz (2015) were able to distinguish individuals with probable AD from individuals without AD using only short samples of their verbal responses on a picture description task. The four features that emerged from the verbal responses were semantic impairment, acoustic abnormality, syntactic impairment, and information impairment. Masrani et al. (2017a) also recently explored the task of automatically detecting evidence of dementia within blog data.

However, the detection of PD using computational linguistics remains a relatively neglected area, particularly when compared to research on the detection of MCI and AD. The automatic detection of PD has tended to look at acoustic features extracted from speech signals (Bocklet et al., 2013; Orozco-Arroyave et al., 2016; Pompili et al., 2017). However, Garcia et al. (2016) note the necessity of extracting linguistic features from text to detect PD. The authors explain that computational linguistics can address many of the limitations currently present in the literature on the PD-associated linguistic impairments. For instance, research on language ability is often conducted in controlled and artificial settings, whereby participants must process arbitrary strings of letters or words (Lieberman et al., 1992; Hochstadt et al., 2006). Moreover, the use of linguistic features is often manually coded by researchers. In manual coding, researchers use their subjective interpretations to rate language use. As an example, Murray (2000) asked PD and Huntingdon's disease individuals to describe a picture. Judges then rated the responses for "informativeness." Garcia and colleagues (2016) explain that computational linguistics can be used to assess naturally produced speech, avoiding the confound of biased human interpretation. Using support vector machines with a leave-one-out cross-validation approach, the authors found that semantic fields and grammatical features detected PD with significant rates in accuracy. Garcia and colleagues (2016) also found that although word repetitions were unable to accurately detect PD diagnoses, repetitions could accurately predict performance on neuropsychological batteries.

Interestingly, findings from the Nun Study reveal that language ability in early adulthood is a reliable predictor of cognitive function in later life. Indeed, Kemper and colleagues (2001) showed that language skills in younger adulthood, as measured by grammatical complexity and idea density in written autobiographies, can predict the likelihood of dementia in older adulthood. Riley et al. (2005) found that low idea density in early life is a significant predictor of later aging pathologies. Specifically, low idea density in young adulthood correlated significantly with older adult cognitive impairment. Post-mortem examinations also revealed an association between early life low idea density and AD-related neuropathology. It thus seems reasonable to assume that linguistic features can also be used to predict general cognitive performance in healthy older adults and older adults with PD. Additionally, it is possible that some typically ageing older adults may have age-related cognitive deficits. We use linguistic features of task descriptions to detect evidence of PD and also to predict general cognitive performance across all three groups of HYA, HOA, and PD.

3 Corpus Description

In this section we describe the two tasks that were used to generate data, as well as the cognitive tests that were measured.

3.1 Script Generation Task

A total of 10 everyday tasks were used in this experiment. An independent panel of five people generated a list of everyday tasks that would not be biased in terms of gender, age and culture. Out of the everyday tasks generated, the 10 tasks most frequently cited were used. Each participant's responses were transcribed using a recording booklet, each of which displayed the individual task at the top of each page. All of the PD participants were recruited at PD support branches where the researchers gave talks on PD, language and cognition. At the end of the talks, the researchers asked for volunteers for their research. If individuals wished to participate in the research, they later contacted the researcher by phone or email.

All of the PD participants were diagnosed by neurologists from the Tayside and Fife medical trusts as having idiopathic PD. The mean number of years since diagnosis of PD was 9.4 (SD = 3.2). The Hoehn and Yahr's (1967) scale of motor impairment revealed three individuals were in stage II (bilateral involvement) and nine were in stage III (mild to moderate disability with impairment to balance). The HOA participants were drawn from an older adult research participant database and the HYA participants were recruited via convenience sampling.

All of the participants were told the title of each of the tasks (e.g. to write and post a letter). The participants were asked to provide sufficient detail to enable someone who was unfamiliar with the task to complete it successfully using the scripts they provided. None of the participants were given any form of constraint or boundary such as not to provide personal information or to only include principal, high-level actions. All of the participants were provided with an example of a script: drying the dishes (pick up the tea-towel, pick up the wet dish from the draining board, rub the tea-towel all over the dish until it is dry and place the dish in the cupboard in its usual place). When the experimenter was satisfied the participant fully understood the instructions, the experiment began.

None of the participants were corrected or aided by the experimenter once the experiment had started, unless the participant forgot the target item. The experiment took between 30 and 60 minutes to complete and all participants were offered a break after each task. All of the participants were debriefed on completion of the experiment.

3.2 Directions Task

In this experiment, the participants were shown a list of 36 destinations. 18 had been rated as being very familiar or familiar to most people and the remaining 18 had been rated as being relatively familiar or unfamiliar to most people. From the list of 36 destinations, the participants were asked to pick five places that they knew exactly how to get to and five places that they knew of but were only relatively familiar with how to get there. The list of destinations was presented to the participants in a random order and not according to their level of familiarity.

The participants were asked to mark the items with an F if they were familiar with them and a U if they were less familiar with them. Once they had marked five of each, the experimenter confirmed their level of familiarity verbally, e.g. "so you are familiar with directions to a vet?" or "so you are not as familiar with the directions to a zoo?"

The participants were then asked to provide directions for each of their choices, with the choices ordered randomly. They were asked to provide as clear and precise directions as possible. All participants were asked to give directions from a point they were most comfortable with, e.g. from their house to the zoo.

Note: Participant recruitment for the directions task was the same as used in the script generation task.

3.3 Demographic Information

Here we briefly describe basic demographic information about the participants across the two tasks. In the PD group, the average age was 64.1 and the group was evenly split between males and females. The HOA group had an average age of 69.1 and featured two males and 15 females. The HYA group had an average age of 27.17 and contained four males and five females. All participants were Caucasian and were British nationals.

3.4 Cognitive and Depression Scores

Here we briefly describe three scores that we analyze in this study: two cognitive scores, and one depression score.

Phonological Abilities Test (PAT)   The PAT is made up of a series of phonological abilities tasks. The PAT was thus designed to identify reading difficulties early on in young children (Muter et al., 1997). The six tests within the PAT are 1. rhyme detection, 2. rhyme production, 3, word completion, 4, phoneme deletion, 5. speech rate and 6. letter knowledge. The first four tests measure phonological awareness. The fifth test measures speech rate (repeating the word buttercup 10 times as quickly as possible) and the sixth measures knowledge of letters (supplying the name or the sound of each of the twenty-six letters of the alphabet). Only the first four phonological awareness tasks were used in the research.

Alternate Uses Test (AUT)   The AUT is a measurement of mental inflexibility. The AUT asks participants to produce as many uses for common objects (e.g. brick, or paper) as they can think of. Providing obvious and conventional uses for objects is thought to reflect convergent thinking. An example is suggesting you can use a brick to build a house or use paper to write a letter. Divergent thinking is, however, reflected in responses such as using a brick to make a sculpture or using paper to make a mask for a ball. The diminished capacity to provide uncommon uses of an object is believed to be symptomatic of the inability to switch from one mental set to another and thus the AUT is often employed as a measure of executive function (Lezak, 2004). In this work, we focus on the AUT uncommon uses score (AUTU).

Beck Depression Inventory (BDI)   The BDI-short consists of 13 items. It is used within a clinical and research setting to measure levels of depression. The BDI is frequently used because it is easy to administer and score. It has the capacity to determine the presence and the level of depression but is unable to measure the frequency and duration of depressive illness (Lezak, 2004). It measures levels of depression by asking the individual to make self-reports about how they are feeling.

4 Experimental Setup

In this section we describe the features, machine learning models, and evaluation metrics used in these experiments.

4.1 Features

We use a wide variety of linguistic features derived from the subjects' transcripts. The features are entirely derived from the transcripts, as the original speech recordings were not preserved. The features fall into the following categories, and for key features we provide a short handle that can be referred to in the results section.

Psycholinguistic   We use several psycholinguistic features. Words are scored for their concreteness (CNC), imageability (IMG), typical age of acquisition (AOA), and familiarity (FAM). We also derive SUBTL scores for words, which indicate how frequently they are used in everyday life (subtl1 and subtl2). Masrani et al. (2017b) found similar features useful for detecting MCI.

Dependency Parse Features   All sentences are parsed using spaCy's dependency parser[1]. We extract several features, including the branching factor of the root of the dependency tree (maxroot_sc), the maximum branching factor of any node in the dependency tree (maxchild_sc), sparse bag-of-relations features, and the type-token ratio for dependency relations (tt_dep).

Sentiment   We use the SO-Cal sentiment lexicon (Taboada et al., 2011), which associates positive and negative scores with sentiment-bearing words, indicating how positive or negative their sentiment typically is. These are summed over sentences, and then averaged over each document.

GloVe Word Vectors   Words are represented using GloVe vectors[2], and the vectors are summed over sentences. We then create a document vector that is the average of the sentence vectors. The first five dimensions of the document vectors are used as features (denoted as vdim1 $\cdots$ vdim5 in later discussion).

Lexical Cohesion   We measure cohesion using the average cosine similarity of adjacent sentences in a document, using the GloVe vectors.

Sentence and Document Length   We include the average number of words per sentence (avelen), and average number of sentences per document (num_sens).

Part-of-Speech Tags   We use spaCy's part-of-speech tagger, and use a sparse bag-of-tags representation for the most frequent tags, as well as the type-token ratio for tags (tt_pos).

Other Lexical Features   Finally, we use a bag-of-words representation for the most common 200 non-stopwords in the dataset, and also calculate the type-token ratio for words (type/token).

4.2 Models and Evaluation

In these experiments we primarily use Random Forest regression and classification models, though in the final set of experiments we compare several machine learning methods, including an ensemble of models. We employ a leave-one-out cross-validation procedure.

In the following section, we report results at two levels. At the *document level*, each data instance is an individual description generated by a subject, and the features are derived from each single description. At the *participant level*, each data instance is a participant (subject) and the features are aggregated over all of that participant's descriptions. When doing prediction at the document level, we ensure that a participant cannot have instances in both the training and testing folds.

For evaluation, we report accuracy scores and compare model accuracy with the baseline accuracy that is achieved when always predicting the majority class. We also report the area under the curve (AUC), where 0.5 indicates random classification performance and 1 is perfect classification performance.

---

[1] `https://spacy.io/`
[2] `https://nlp.stanford.edu/projects/glove/`

Model	AUC	Acc.
Random Forest	0.913	0.927
Baseline	0.5	0.78

Table 1: Predicting Younger vs. Older

5   Experimental Results

In this section we describe the sequence of experiments we carried out, with both positive and negative results.

5.1   Binary Classification of Parkinson's Disease

Our first experiment demonstrates the difficulty of treating the automatic detection of PD as a binary classification task. We treat the healthy older adults (HOA) and healthy younger adults (HYA) as a single class (the non-PD class) and subjects with PD as the other class (PD). The goal is to use the extracted linguistic features to detect evidence of PD, at both the document level and participant level.

However, at both the document level and participant level, the classification results are essentially random, with AUC scores of 0.49 and 0.51, respectively. Similarly, accuracy levels are below the baseline performance of a system that simply predicts the majority class. We analyze this result in the next set of experiments.

5.2   Binary Classification of Older vs. Younger Cohorts

One interpretation of the negative results from the previous section is that the task is difficult because of linguistic similarities between healthy older adults and older adults with PD, and that the cohort of healthy younger adults is linguistically distinct from both older groups.

To test this, we trained a new binary classification model to predict younger vs. older subjects. One class contains the HYA cohort and the other class contains HOA + PD subjects.

The results support our hypothesis, with extremely high accuracy in discriminating between younger and older subjects. Table 1 shows the participant-level prediction scores, with an AUC score of 0.913 using the random forest regression model. The two older groups are highly similar to one another in many respects, with the younger cohort being distinct.

Figures 1 and 2 show some of the similarities between the two older groups and that the younger group is distinct; specifically, the healthy younger adults show higher sentiment and higher SUBTL scores, and the two older groups are similar to each other in terms of those features. This pattern is reflected in many of the other features as well, e.g. younger adults have higher syntactic complexity and lower type-token ratios than the older group.

Given the positive results on this task, we next move away from treating the healthy older adults and healthy younger adults as a single group, and move towards employing a machine learning model that can separate age-related language differences from language differences relating to PD.

5.3   Multi-Class Prediction: Healthy Younger, Healthy Older, and Subjects with Parkinson's

Based on the results of the previous two sets of experiments, we reformulated the problem as a multi-class prediction, with three distinct classes HYA, HOA, and PD. We again use the same set of linguistic features described earlier, and random forest classification models. We report accuracy but not AUC scores since this is no longer a binary classification task.

Table 2 summarizes the accuracy scores for document-level and participant-level prediction. Document-level prediction is only at baseline levels, which is not surprising given that many of the documents are very short (some are 1-2 sentences). However, prediction at the participant-level is substantially better than baseline performance, with an overall accuracy of 0.63.

Summarizing the results so far, the first experiment illustrates the difficulty of treating PD detection as a binary classification task. The second experiment explains why, showing that healthy older adults and subjects with PD have linguistic similarities, while healthy younger adults are distinct. This third

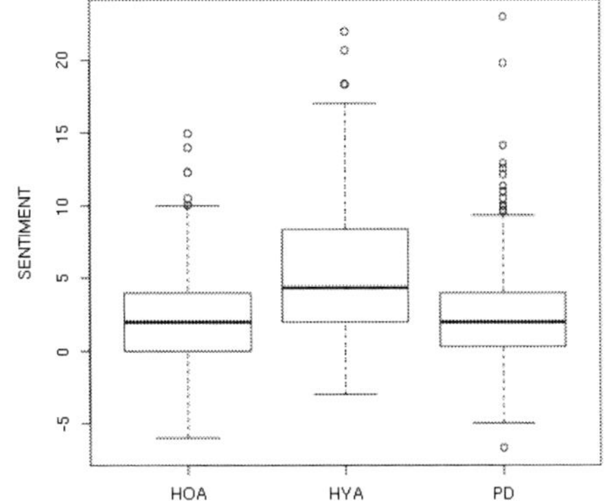

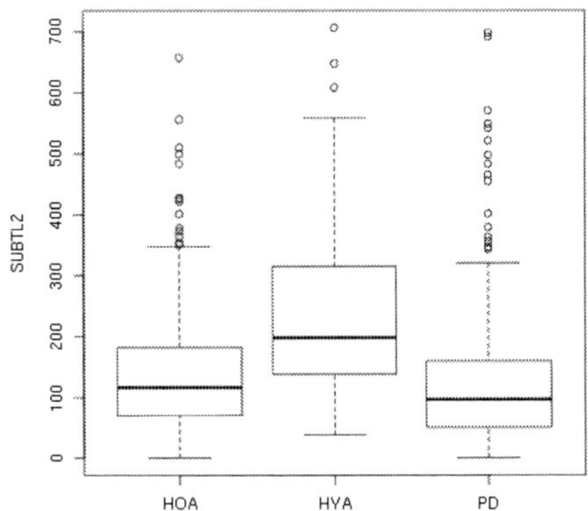

Figure 1: Sentiment by Group   Figure 2: SUBTL2 Scores by Group

Model	Document-Level	Participant-Level
Random Forest	0.52	0.63
Baseline	0.54	0.41

Table 2: Accuracy for Multi-Class Prediction

experiment shows that performance is substantially better than baseline performance when approaching the task as a multi-class problem.

5.4 Prediction of Cognitive and Depression Scores

Our final set of experiments moves beyond the prediction of discrete classes, and we instead try to predict the cognitive abilities of all subjects in all cohorts. This is motivated partly by the above experimental results, and by the hypothesis that some healthy older adults might have mild age-related cognitive impairment, even though they have not been diagnosed with PD or any form of dementia.

As described in Section 3, we recorded a variety of cognitive and depression measures for each subject. In this final experiment, we test whether we can use the same linguistic features as the previous experiments for predicting cognitive and depression scores across all participants.

Table 3 summarizes the results for automatic prediction of three of the test scores, BDI, AUTU, and PAT. For both BDI and PAT, the best machine learning models are able to outperform a baseline that predicts the mean value of the training observations. The ensemble of models yields the lowest MSE on predicting BDI scores, while the Lasso and Random Forest regression methods give the lowest MSE on predicting PAT scores. On predicting AUTU scores, no machine learning model fares better than the baseline. This is owing to the fact that there is relatively little variation in scores amongst subjects. For BDI, the ensemble approach gives results that are significantly better than kNN and Random Forests,

Model	BDI	AUTU	PAT
Least Squares	7.46	226.26	166.81
Lasso	7.37	112.51	**75.92**
kNN	8.69	100.37	95.32
Random Forest	8.89	83.53	82.21
Ensemble	**6.69**	98.35	76.60
Baseline	8.25	**82.54**	94.21

Table 3: MSE for Predicting Cognitive and Depression Scores

Variable	SS	df	MSE	F	P
BDI	113.74	2,38	56.87	10.38**	.00
PA	1591.10	2,38	795.55	15.44**	.00
AUTU	1112.08	2,38	556.04	11.91**	.00

Note. N=41. *p<.05, **p<.01

Table 4: A One-Way Analysis of Variance of Neuropsychology Test Scores by Group

	HYA vs. HOA			HYA vs. PD			PD vs. HOA		
Variable	Mean Diff.	SE	p	Mean Diff.	SE	p	Mean Diff.	SE	p
avelen	1.27	1.31	.60	4.34**	1.36	.01	-3.07*	1.19	.04
sentiment	3.26**	.74	.00	2.59**	.77	.01	.67	.67	.58
vdim1	-3.85*	1.49	.04	-.22	1.55	.99	-3.63*	1.35	.03
vdim4	-1.23	.61	.12	.36	.63	.84	-1.58*	.55	.02

Note. *p<.05, **p<.01

Table 5: Tukey HSD Post Hoc Comparisons of Group for Average Length of Script, Sentiment, Vdim1 & Vdim4

according to paired t-tests. For AUT, the only statistically significant differences are that least squares regression is significantly worse than the Random Forests, Lasso, ensemble, and baseline approaches. For PAT, the ensemble and Lasso approaches are again significantly better than least squares regression.

Figures 3, 4, and 5 show feature importance scores for some of the features that were most useful in predicting AUTU, BDI, and PAT, respectively. An individual feature's importance score is determined by how useful that feature was in reducing MSE, on average, when it was used as a split in the decisions trees used within the Random Forests model. For example, length and sentiment features are very useful for all three prediction tasks.

We also perform statistical analyses to further explore linguistic ability and cognitive functioning. First, a one-way Analysis of Variance (ANOVA) was used to examine an effect of group (3 levels: HYA, HOA & PD) on the cognitive tests, as illustrated in Table 4. Analyses revealed main effects of group on BDI scores (F (2, 38) = 10.38, $p < .01$), PAT scores, (F (2, 38) = 15.44, $p < .01$), and AUTU scores (F (2, 38) = 11.91, $p < .01$). The results indicate that group has a significant effect on all three of the cognitive tests.

A one-way ANOVA was also used to examine an effect of group on the linguistic features. Analyses revealed main effects of group on average length of script (F (2, 38) = 5.81, $p = .01$, $\eta^2 = .23$), sentiment (F (2, 38) = 10.15, $p < .01$, $\eta^2 = .35$), vdim1 (F (2, 38) = 4.92, $p = .01$, $\eta^2 = .21$), and vdim4 (F (2, 38) = 4.53, $p = .02$, $\eta^2 = .19$). Post hoc comparisons were performed using the Tukey HSD test, as illustrated in Table 5. Tukey HSD comparisons revealed significant differences between the groups for the following measures ($p < .05$): average length of scripts was significantly lower in the PD group ($M = 13.60$, $SD = 2.69$) compared to the HOA group ($M = 16.67$, $SD = 3.74$) and the HYA group ($M = 17.93$, $SD = 3.20$). The number of sentiment items was also significantly higher in the HYA group ($M = 5.40$, $SD = 2.51$) than the HOA group ($M = 2.51$, $SD = 1.02$) and the PD group ($M = 2.82$, $SD = 2.09$). The HOA group had greater mean vdim1 values ($M = 6.91$, $SD = 4.64$) than the HYA group ($M = 3.06$, $SD = 1.20$) and the PD group ($M = 3.28$, $SD = 3.69$). Finally, mean vdim4 values were significantly lower in the PD group ($M = -.34$, $SD = .81$) than the HOA group ($M = 1.25$, $SD = 1.58$).

Spearman's rank correlation coefficients were performed to measure correlations between the linguistic features observed in the scripts and the cognitive assessment scores. Correlations were performed within each group. While there were no significant correlations within the HYA and HOA group, significant correlations did emerge in the PD group. The AUTU score formed positive correlations with the features vdim4 ($r_s = .79$, $p < .01$) and vdim1 ($r_s = .74$, $p < .01$). Moreover, scores on the BDI were negatively correlated with the feature vdim1 ($r_s = -.76$, $p < .01$).

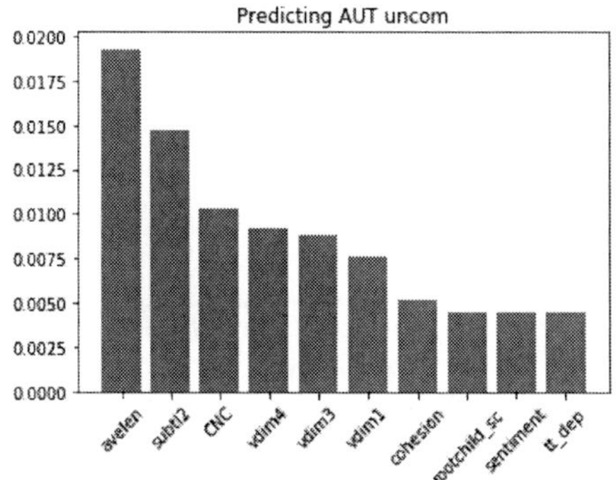

Figure 3: Feature Importance: AUTU

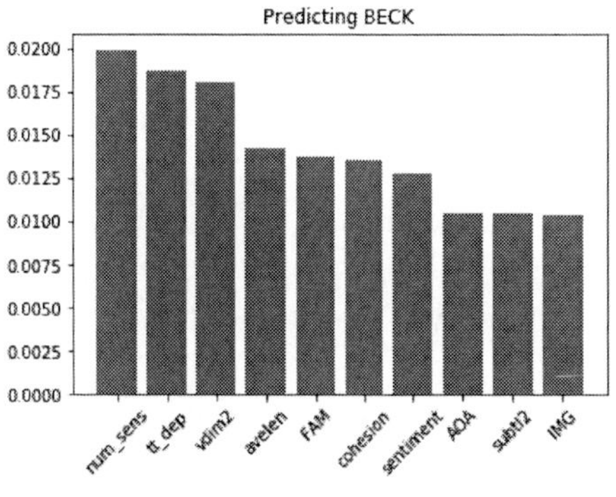

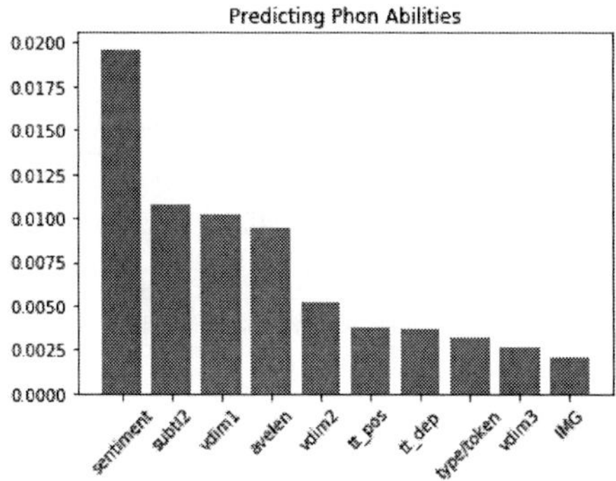

Figure 4: Feature Importance: BDI

Figure 5: Feature Importance: PAT

6   Conclusion

In this set of experiments, we have used natural language processing and machine learning to automatically detect evidence of PD in task transcripts generated by subjects. We first showed that it is difficult to approach this as a binary classification task, particularly because of linguistic similarities between healthy older adults and older adults with PD. We subsequently showed that a multi-class classification approach yields better results. Finally, we used the same set of linguistic features to predict scores of cognitive ability across all subjects.

The vast majority of previous work on automatically detecting Parkinson's disease from speech has focused on using acoustic features. Like Garcia et al. (2016), we demonstrated that linguistic features can be very useful for this task. In future work where we have both speech recordings and transcripts, we will investigate the use of multi-modal features.

Future work will also include further experiments on automatically predicting cognitive ability scores, as we have collected numerous other cognitive measures for the subjects who participated in these tasks.

References

Wendy L Arnott, Helen J Chenery, Bruce E Murdoch, and Peter A Silburn. 2005. Morphosyntactic and syntactic priming: an investigation of underlying processing mechanisms and the effects of parkinson's disease. *Journal of Neurolinguistics*, 18(1):1–28.

Tobias Bocklet, Stefan Steidl, Elmar Nöth, and Sabine Skodda. 2013. Automatic evaluation of parkinsons speech-acoustic, prosodic and voice related cues. In *Proc. of Interspeech, Lyon, France*.

F Boller, Albert M. L., and F Denes. 1975. Palilalia. *British Journal of Disorders of Communication*, 10:92–97.

E Bora, M Walterfang, and D Velakoulis. 2015. Theory of mind in parkinson's disease: A meta-analysis. *Behavioural Brain Research*, 292:515–520.

J Bottcher. 1975. Morphology of the basal ganglia in parkinson's disease. *Acta Neurologica Scandinavica*, 52:7–87.

F. L Darley, A. E Aronson, and J. R Brown. 1975. Hypokinetic dysarthria. pages 171–197.

M. C deRijk, L. J Launer, K Berger, M. M Breteler, J. F Dartigues, M Baldereschi, and A Hofman. 2000. Prevalence of parkinsons disease in europe: A collaborative study of population-based cohorts. *Neurology*, 54:S21–S23.

Georg Dirnberger and Marjan Jahanshahi. 2013. Executive dysfunction in parkinson's disease: a review. *Journal of neuropsychology*, 7(2):193–224.

Bruno Dubois. 1991. Cognitive deficits in parkinson's disease. *Handbook of neuropsychology*, 5:195–240.

Kathleen C Fraser, Jed A Meltzer, and Frank Rudzicz. 2015. Linguistic features identify alzheimers disease in narrative speech. *Journal of Alzheimer's Disease*, 49(2):407–422.

John DE Gabrieli, Jaswinder Singh, Glenn T Stebbins, and Christopher G Goetz. 1996. Reduced working memory span in parkinson's disease: Evidence for the role of frontostriatal system in working and strategic memory. *Neuropsychology*, 10(3):322.

Adolfo M García, Facundo Carrillo, Juan Rafael Orozco-Arroyave, Natalia Trujillo, Jesús F Vargas Bonilla, Sol Fittipaldi, Federico Adolfi, Elmar Nöth, Mariano Sigman, Diego Fernández Slezak, et al. 2016. How language flows when movements dont: an automated analysis of spontaneous discourse in parkinsons disease. *Brain and language*, 162:19–28.

Jeremy Gauntlett-Gilbert, Richard C Roberts, and Verity J Brown. 1999. Mechanisms underlying attentional set-shifting in parkinsons disease. *Neuropsychologia*, 37(5):605–616.

Murray Grossman, Susan Carvell, Matthew B Stern, Stephen Gollomp, and Howard I Hurtig. 1992. Sentence comprehension in parkinson's disease: The role of attention and memory. *Brain and language*, 42(4):347–384.

Murray Grossman, Jenifer Mickanin, Keith M Robinson, and Mark D'Esposito. 1996. Anomaly judgments of subject–predicate relations in alzheimer's disease. *Brain and Language*, 54(2):216–232.

Murray Grossman, Julia Kalmanson, Nechama Bernhardt, Jennifer Morris, Matthew B Stern, and Howard I Hurtig. 2000. Cognitive resource limitations during sentence comprehension in parkinson's disease. *Brain and Language*, 73(1):1–16.

JM Gurd and RM Oliveira. 1996. Competitive inhibition models of lexical–semantic processing: Experimental evidence. *Brain and Language*, 54(3):414–433.

Julie D Henry and John R Crawford. 2004. Verbal fluency deficits in parkinson's disease: a meta-analysis. *Journal of the International Neuropsychological Society*, 10(4):608–622.

Jesse Hochstadt, Hiroko Nakano, Philip Lieberman, and Joseph Friedman. 2006. The roles of sequencing and verbal working memory in sentence comprehension deficits in parkinsons disease. *Brain and language*, 97(3):243–257.

Margaret M Hoehn, Melvin D Yahr, et al. 1967. Parkinsonism: onset, progression, and mortality. *Neurology*, 50(2):318–318.

Judy Illes. 1989. Neurolinguistic features of spontaneous language production dissociate three forms of neurodegenerative disease: Alzheimer's, huntington's, and parkinson's. *Brain and language*, 37(4):628–642.

David Kemmerer. 1999. Impaired comprehension of raising-to-subject constructions in parkinson's disease. *Brain and Language*, 66(3):311–328.

Susan Kemper, Lydia H Greiner, Janet G Marquis, Katherine Prenovost, and Tracy L Mitzner. 2001. Language decline across the life span: findings from the nun study. *Psychology and aging*, 16(2):227.

Yvan Lebrun. 1996. Cluttering after brain damage. *Journal of Fluency Disorders*, 21(3-4):289–295.

Eun-Young Lee, Nelson Cowan, Edward K Vogel, Terry Rolan, Fernando Valle-Inclan, and Steven A Hackley. 2010. Visual working memory deficits in patients with parkinson's disease are due to both reduced storage capacity and impaired ability to filter out irrelevant information. *Brain*, 133(9):2677–2689.

Muriel Deutsch Lezak. 2004. *Neuropsychological assessment*. Oxford University Press, USA.

Philip Lieberman, Edward Kako, Joseph Friedman, Gary Tajchman, Liane S Feldman, and Elsa B Jiminez. 1992. Speech production, syntax comprehension, and cognitive deficits in parkinson's disease. *Brain and language*, 43(2):169–189.

Vaden Masrani, Gabriel Murray, Thalia Field, and Giuseppe Carenini. 2017a. Detecting dementia through retrospective analysis of routine blog posts by bloggers with dementia. *BioNLP 2017*, pages 232–237.

Vaden Masrani, Gabriel Murray, Thalia Field, and Giuseppe Carenini. 2017b. Domain adaptation for detecting mild cognitive impairment. In *Proc. of Canadian AI, Edmonton, Canada*.

Rena Matison, Richard Mayeux, Jeffrey Rosen, and Stanley Fahn. 1982. tip-of-the-tongue phenomenon in parkinson disease. *Neurology*, 32(5):567–567.

Patrick McNamara and Raymon Durso. 2003. Pragmatic communication skills in patients with parkinsons disease. *Brain and language*, 84(3):414–423.

Patrick McNamara, Loraine K Obler, Rhoda Au, Raymon Durso, and Martin L Albert. 1992. Speech monitoring skills in alzheimer's disease, parkinson's disease, and normal aging. *Brain and Language*, 42(1):38–51.

Laura L Murray. 2000. Spoken language production in huntington's and parkinson's diseases. *Journal of Speech, Language, and Hearing Research*, 43(6):1350–1366.

Valerie Muter, Charles Hulme, and Margaret J Snowling. 1997. *The phonological abilities test*. The Psychological Corporation.

Dimitris Natsopoulos, Z Katsarou, S Bostantzopoulou, George Grouios, G Mentenopoulos, and J Logothetis. 1991. Strategies in comprehension of relative clauses by parkinsonian patients. *Cortex*, 27(2):255–268.

John G Nutt, John P Hammerstad, and Stephen T Gancher. 1992. *Parkinson's disease: 100 maxims*. Mosby Inc.

JR Orozco-Arroyave, F Hönig, JD Arias-Londoño, JF Vargas-Bonilla, K Daqrouq, S Skodda, J Rusz, and E Nöth. 2016. Automatic detection of parkinson's disease in running speech spoken in three different languages. *The Journal of the Acoustical Society of America*, 139(1):481–500.

Anna Pompili, Alberto Abad, Paolo Romano, Isabel P Martins, Rita Cardoso, Helena Santos, Joana Carvalho, Isabel Guimarães, and Joaquim J Ferreira. 2017. Automatic detection of parkinsons disease: An experimental analysis of common speech production tasks used for diagnosis. In *International Conference on Text, Speech, and Dialogue*, pages 411–419. Springer.

Christopher Randolph, Allen R Braun, Terry E Goldberg, and Thomas N Chase. 1993. Semantic fluency in alzheimer's, parkinson's, and huntington's disease: Dissociation of storage and retrieval failures. *Neuropsychology*, 7(1):82.

Kathryn P Riley, David A Snowdon, Mark F Desrosiers, and William R Markesbery. 2005. Early life linguistic ability, late life cognitive function, and neuropathology: findings from the nun study. *Neurobiology of aging*, 26(3):341–347.

Brian Roark, Margaret Mitchell, John-Paul Hosom, Kristy Hollingshead, and Jeffrey Kaye. 2011. Spoken language derived measures for detecting mild cognitive impairment. *IEEE Transactions on Audio, Speech, and Language Processing*, 19(7):2081–2090.

A Samii, J Nutt, and B Ransom. 2004. Parkinson's disease. *The Lancet*, 363(9423):1783–1793.

Maite Taboada, Julian Brooke, Milan Tofiloski, Kimberly Voll, and Manfred Stede. 2011. Lexicon-based methods for sentiment analysis. *Computational linguistics*, 37(2):267–307.

Michael T Ullman, Suzanne Corkin, Marie Coppola, Gregory Hickok, John H Growdon, Walter J Koroshetz, and Steven Pinker. 1997. A neural dissociation within language: Evidence that the mental dictionary is part of declarative memory, and that grammatical rules are processed by the procedural system. *Journal of cognitive neuroscience*, 9(2):266–276.

Sonja von Campenhausen, Bornschein Bernhard, Wick Regina, Bötzel Kai, Sampaio Cristina, Poewe Werner, Oertel Wolfgang, Siebert Uwe, Berger Karin, and Dodel Richard. 2005. Prevalence and incidence of parkinson's disease in europe. *European Neuropsychopharmacology*, 15(4):473–490.

Ronald F Zec, Edward S Landreth, Sally Fritz, Eugenia Grames, Ann Hasara, Wade Fraizer, James Belman, Stacy Wainman, Matthew McCool, Carolyn OConnell, et al. 1999. A comparison of phonemic, semantic, and alternating word fluency in parkinsons disease. *Archives of Clinical Neuropsychology*, 14(3):255–264.

Guohua Zhao, Feiyan Chen, Qiong Zhang, Mowei Shen, and Zaifeng Gao. 2018. Feature-based information filtering in visual working memory is impaired in parkinson's disease. *Neuropsychologia*.

Can spontaneous spoken language disfluencies help describe syntactic dependencies? An empirical study

M. Zakaria KURDI
Department of Computer Science, University of Lynchburg,
Lynchburg, VA
kurdi_m@lynchburg.eduAbstract

Abstract

This paper explores the correlations between key syntactic dependencies and the occurrence of simple spoken language disfluencies such as filled pauses and incomplete words. The working hypothesis here is that interruptions caused by these phenomena are more likely to happen between weakly connected words from a syntactic point of view than between strongly connected ones. The obtained results show significant patterns with the regard to key syntactic phenomena, like confirming the positive correlation between the frequency of disfluencies and multiples measures of syntactic complexity. In addition, they show that there is a stronger relationship between the verb and its subject than with its object, which confirms the idea of a hierarchical incrementality. Also, this work uncovered an interesting role played by a verb particle as a syntactic delimiter of some verb complements. Finally, the interruptions by disfluencies patterns show that verbs have a more privileged relationship with their preposition compared to the object Noun Phrase (NP).

1 Introduction

This paper explores the way speech stream is interrupted by *simple spoken language disfluencies* (from now disfluencies) such as filled pauses and incomplete words (Kurdi, 2016). It aims to shed light on language planning during the language generation process through the window of disfluencies. One of the key questions this work tries to answer is how tightly related are some syntactic components within an utterance. The underlying hypothesis here is that tightly related components are planned together and consequently less likely interrupted by a disfluency.

Another contribution of this work is to provide a numeric value to describe the strength of the linguistic connection between two words, as this study is conducted at the scale of an entire corpus. Please note that the linguistic and cognitive validity of the existing statistical models to describe the strength of a dependency, based on the co-occurrence of words and structures, is highly disputed by many linguists like Chomsky. A basic argument against such models is that a rare structure can be as grammatical as a frequently used one. Hence, the potential applications of this work within the area of NLP can range from syntactic disambiguation to the reranking of speech recognition N best hypotheses.

In previous research, disfluencies were explored from multiple points of views. For example, (Carbonell and Hayes, 1984), (Heeman, 1999), (Core, 1999), and (Kurdi, 2002) investigated this relation within the context of spoken language parsing. In the psycholinguistics literature, several models stressed the role of syntax in the process of language production and planning. For instance, serial processing models of language production such as Fromkin's five stage model (Fromkin, 1973), Garrett's model (Garrett, 1980), (Garrett, 1988), and Bock and Levelt's model (Bock and Levelt, 1994) assume the existence of an explicit module for syntactic processing to which they attribute different names and functional roles. In connectionists models, such as Dells' model (Dell et al, 1999), all knowledge levels interact with each other, with the lexicon playing a central role in this process. When a word is selected all the phonological, morphological and syntactic features related to its constituents are also activated and propagated to the context, contributing to activate new words. This suggests that syntactic dependencies between words play a key role in the process of spoken language production.

Besides, several previous works stipulate that self-monitoring plays a key role in language production. In particular, Levelt's Perceptual Loop Theory (PLT) suggests that there exist two modes of monitoring

Proceedings of the First International Workshop on Language Cognition and Computational Models, pages 75–84
Santa Fe, New Mexico, United States, August 20, 2018.
https://doi.org/10.18653/v1/P17

(Levelt, 1983). The first one consists of monitoring internal unproduced speech which consists of checking one's planned formulation silently. Similar to the process of listening to other's speech, the external monitoring, on the other hand, consists of monitoring one's speech by ears. Both processes, involve treatment by the speech comprehension system, which covers both the semantic and syntactic aspects of language. Some more recent works such as the ones of (Nozari, Dell, & Schwartz, 2011) and (Hartsuiker and Herman, 2001) argue for internal monitoring based on competition between representations within the language production system without the intervention of the comprehension system. It is hard to see how these new studies can contradict the idea of the intervention of syntax within the monitoring system for the following reasons. First, these studies focused on low-level linguistic phenomena such as word production and do not take into consideration the syntactic structure. In addition, self-repair can be motivated to correct syntactic errors. Likewise, many works have indicated that discourse, syntax, and prosody play an important role within language planning (see (Wagner, 2016) for a review of these works).

Furthermore, multiple works have shown that there is a correlation between language complexity in general and production of disfluency (McLaughlin and Cullinan, 1989), (Haynes, Hood, 1978). More specifically, syntactic complexity is linked to frequency of production of disfluencies (Gordon and Luper, 1989), (Logan and Lasalle, 1999) disfluency initiation times (Ferreira, 1991). Besides, (Boomer, 1965) reported that filled pauses tend to appear between the first and the second word of a clause, suggesting that this may be related to the syntactic planning of the utterance. Some other works focused on syntactic planning and disfluency within the context of foreign language (Rose, 2017).

A question one could ask about the generation, the planning or the monitoring processes is the following. Which syntactic unit is used by these processes? Some studies suggested that clause (or simple sentence) plays a key role in this process (Ford and Holmes, 1978), (Rose, 2017), while others stipulated that structures like LTAG trees are used (Ferreira, 2000). In addition, Levelt, in his extension of Dell's three level model, assumes that the grammar encoding is done within the lemma-stratum module where processing is based on syntactic features of individual words such as tense for the verbs (Levelt et al, 1999).

2 Methodology

2.1 Hypotheses

The working assumption in this paper is that the locations of the interruptions of speech flow by disfluencies are related to the syntactic dependencies within the utterance. For example, if the interruption happens rarely within a given context (e.g. between two morphological categories, like a determiner and a noun DT NN) we assume that the components involved in this context are strongly connected and vice versa.

This fundamental assumption leads to the following four hypotheses:

i. Disfluencies are the reflection of a heavy cognitive processing (Lindström, 2008). Hence, it is more likely that disfluencies occur in a more syntactically complex utterance.

ii. Given their shared features, verbs are more tightly connected to their subject than to their object. This means that it is less likely to observe an interruption between a verb and its subject than between a verb and its object.

iii. The relation between particles and verbs is so tight morphologically. From a semantic point of view, a particle may change the meaning of some verbs. In addition, it is hypothesized here that verb particles play a key syntactic role in planning and delimiting some of the verb arguments.

iv. Given the privileged relationship between the verb and its preposition, it is hypothesized that interruptions between the verb and the preposition are less likely than between the preposition and the subsequent Noun Phrase (NP).

2.2 Corpus

The Trains Corpus (Heeman and Allen, 1995) was used because of the quality of transcription and reasonable size: 98 dialogues with 34 different speakers and 5,900 speaker turns. Unlike other spoken language corpora, the task is complex which creates more opportunities for producing disfluencies. After a comparative study with a portion of the switchboard corpus (Meteer, 1995), it was possible to observe that the disfluencies available in the Trains Corpus are similar to the ones in the Switchboard Corpus.

2.3 Data annotation

The disfluencies are annotated using the scheme adopted in (Kurdi, 2003). Given that the focus of this work is about syntax, are adopted the following criteria for defining an interruption of the utterance flow. First, filled pauses and incomplete words such as *hum* and *prob-* are the obvious indicators. Some prosodic events such as silence (unfilled pauses) were not considered. The problem with silence is that it is hard to mark with high accuracy given the individual differences between speakers' pace. Also, speakers may take a short pause for the sake of breathing, a rather physiological event. Finally, silence markers are likely to be accompanied by one or more of the adopted interruption indicators. Are also excluded contextual and physiological events such as breadth and laugher as they are not necessarily related to language planning.

2.4 Interruption rate

To provide a probability-like measure of the connectivity rate, Interruption Rate (IR) is adopted. It is calculated using equation 1 where $c(x)$ means the count of x:

$$\text{interruption\_rate(n-gram}_i) = \frac{c(\text{interrupted n-gram}_i)}{c(\text{all occurences of n-gram}_i)} \quad (1)$$

To observe the interruption patterns, two programs are implemented. A statistical part-of-speech (POS) tagger based on a cascade of n-grams trained on the Penn tree bank. To correct the errors with this tagger, is also implemented a post-processing module. It corrects two types of errors: generic and corpus specific errors. For example, is used a rule that would retag all the auxiliary verbs as MD when they are used before a verb. An example of a corpus specific error is the word *Corning* which is only used in the corpus as a proper noun (a city in the state of New York) but the statistical tagger sometimes tags it as a verb. The tag set adopted is inspired by the Penn treebank[1].

The implemented program provides a *raw* interruption rate. Given that n-grams provide only a sequencing of POS tags, which does not necessarily reflect a relation of dependency, all the sequences are checked *manually*. Are considered as *syntactic* interruptions only those that occur between syntactically related words. For example, in the sequence (DT NN VB) such as the one in *okay so just a second **uh** let me see -what time (...)*. The interruption here, by the filled pause *uh*, is not between syntactically dependent words as the sequence *a second* belongs to a different utterance and is not a subject or an object of the verb *see*. Therefore, it is not counted as a syntactic interruption. However, in the sequence (DT NN VB) in *we do not have two trains uh trying to cross (..)* there is a syntactic interruption as *two trains* is the subject of the verb *trying*.

The IR of a specific bigram is compared to the IR of the general bigram (XX), which is .026. The bigram (XX) is made with average IR of all observed sequences of two POS tags in the corpus. Similarly, the IR of a specific trigram is compared to the interruption of the IR of the general trigram pattern (XXX), which is .049.

3 Results

3.1 Disfluencies and utterance syntactic complexity

Several works in the literature have reported that the chance of disfluency production increases with the increase of conceptual or linguistic difficulty of the utterance. In this study, five different measures of syntactic complexity were considered and their correlation with the number of disfluencies within the utterance was calculated (see (Kurdi, 2017) for more information about these measures). The measures involving phrases and the depth of the parsing tree were calculated with the Sandford parser[2].

As seen in Table 1, the syntactic complexity indices and the number of disfluencies have a statistically significant positive correlation, meaning increases in syntactic complexity of an utterance were correlated with increases in the number of disfluencies. The smallest correlation is with the number of

---

[1] https://www.ling.upenn.edu/courses/Fall_2003/ling001/penn_treebank_pos.html
[2] https://nlp.stanford.edu/software/lex-parser.shtml

VB while the largest is with the length of the utterance. This difference between the two correlations remains limited, as it is about 14% of the total value.

Complexity measure	Pearson's correlation with the number of disfluencies
Number of phrases in the utterance	.286
Depth of parsing tree of the utterance	.249
Mean length of the phrases	.276
Number of verbal phrases	.247
Length of the utterance	.289

Table 1 Correlations between the number of disfluencies per utterance and five indices of syntactic complexity, for all the correlations [N=5020, p<.0001]

3.2 Connectivity between the verb and its subject and object

In English, where the canonical order is Subject-Verb-Object (SVO), the verb is the heart of the sentence. The relation between the verb and its subject is privileged because of their shared syntactic features, as they agree in number. The question now is the following. What is the effect of this privileged relationship on the strength of the dependency between the verb and its subject? To answer this question, a two-fold process was carried out. First, the left and right connectivity of the verb is calculated through the patterns (X VB) and (VB X). The first pattern measures the connectivity of any POS tag followed by the verb and the second measures the connectivity of the verb and any POS tag that comes after it. The results show that the verb is slightly more connected to the left than to the right, as the IR of the two patterns is respectively .013, .020 [χ^2= 15.052, p =<.0001, d=.060, 99% CI [.975, .983]].

Given that not all words preceding a verb are the subject nor a part of it and that not all the ones following it are the object nor a part of it, we need a closer investigation. Hence, was carried out an analysis of the IR of the verb and the different syntactic structures that can play the role of subject as well as the same structures in the role of object.

As a global observation, the IR of the individual structures do not give a clear picture of the differences given their small values. For example, with personal pronouns, one of the simplest forms that a verb subject can take (1.a), the IR of the bigram (PPS VB) is equal to .002. The same IR is observed with personal pronouns used as object (2.a).

(1)   a.   so **I guess** all the boxcars will have …
        b.   **the oranges are** at Corning …
        c.   **the shortest route is** via Dansville …

As for the multiword NP, like the pattern (DT NN VB) (1.b), it has an IR that is equal to .059. Concerning the subject sequence (DT JJ NN VB), as in (1.c), the IR rate is equal to .043. Similarly, the IR between the verb and object noun (VB NN) as in (2.b) is .041. Within a similar structure, but with an adjective before the noun (VB JJ NN) (2.c), the IR is equal to .023. The same goes for the sequence (VB DT NN) like in (2.d) where the IR is .050 and the sequence (VB DT JJ NN) (2.e) where IR is .028.

(2)   a.   no you can **carry them** both …
        b.   .. we need to **get oranges** to Elmira …
        c.   … we could **attach both boxcars** to one engine …
        d.   **wait a second** I thought well …
        e.   okay **determine the maximum number** of boxcars

As for indirect complements, where a preposition is necessary to link the verb to its object, we have the trigram (VB IN NN) like in (3.a) with an IR equal to .046. While for a complement preposition phrase (VB IN DT NN) like in (3.c), the IR is .028. Besides, the IR of a verb followed by an indirect object pronoun (VB IN PPO) (3.d) is equal to 0 (we only have 12 occurrences of this pattern). Similar observations were made in the case of verbs requiring a particle (VB RP NN) (3.b), where the IR between the particle and the noun is .018 (no interruptions were observed between the verb and the particle).

(3)   a.   … the ones that we **filled with bananas**…

b.   ... **pick up oranges** for that one ...

c.   ... as **shown on the map** ...

d.   no they are already **waiting for me** ...

Nevertheless, the overall interruption rate of subject structures, which is equal to .004, is about six times smaller than the interruption rate of object structures, which is .025. The difference here is statistically significant [χ^2= 54.182, p =<.0001, d=.177, 99% CI = [.974, .966]]. Please note that the effect size (*Cohen d*) cannot be big with disfluencies, given their small frequency.

3.3   Verb, particles, and prepositions

Particles are a class of invariant words that are used to change the semantics of some verbs (Malmkjaer, 2002). Their behavior is very close to the prepositions'. Some of their notable syntactic properties are worth to discuss, however. The main difference between a particle and a preposition provided in grammar manuals is that a preposition always comes before the NP. For example, it comes directly before the noun like in (4.d), before the determiner in an NP (4.e), or before a proper noun (4.f).

(4)   a.   ... try and **work this out** ...

b.   and **bring it over** to Corning ...

c.   ... if I **drive the engine up** from Avon to Dansville ...

d.   so that is **from engine** E two ...

e.   work **at the same** time right

f.   I can get **to Bath** by seven ...

On the other hand, a particle can be moved around a noun, a demonstrative pronoun (4.a), object pronoun complement (4.b), or an NP complement with a determiner and a noun (4.c). In this case, the particle that behaves like a separate morpheme of the verb can be dislocated some words away from it. The hypothesis here is that all the constituents that are embedded between the verb and its particles are planned together. Please note that some verbs admit both a particle and a preposition (5.b).

During this study, eight backward patterns were identified (connections with words at the left-hand context) with 631 occurrences and eleven forward ones (connections with words to the right-hand context) with 607 occurrences. The IR of the backward patterns is 0 (out of a total of 628 cases), while the IR of the forward ones is .029. This shows that, in general, the particles play the role of an argument to a previous word rather than a predicate or argument with relation to the following word.

The data show no interruptions between the verb and the following particle (VB RP) (5.a). The difference between the general pattern XX (general bigram) with the pattern VB RP is statistically significant [χ^2= 13.389, p= <.001, d= .2328, 99% CI= [.971, .975]]. A similar pattern between the verb and the following particle and preposition (VB RP IN) is observed as in (5.b). When followed by a preposition only without a particle (VB IN), the IR is .006. Comparing this pattern to the general pattern XX gives also significant results but a smaller effect size than with VB RP [χ^2= 34.2988, p=<.001, d=.1562, 99% CI = [.971, .974]].

(5)   a.   to Avon to **pick up** the bananas

b.   okay so it is **starting out with** a boxcar

c.   I guess **by train**

To demonstrate the syntactic role of the RP after a verb, other patterns involving a verb followed by an RP have also been depicted. Interestingly, the patterns (VB RP IN) has zero interruption rate as well. As for the cases involving a verb, a particle and another POS in between, were identified two major trigrams with the categories PPO (e.g, *it, them*) and PRON (e.g. *this, those, that*). Besides, nine minor trigram structures involving categories such as CD (e.g. *one*), RB (e.g. *back, only, already*), and NPP (e.g. *Bath*) are also identified. These patterns have frequencies ranging from one to six cases. If we take the general pattern (VB X RP), where X is a category among the previously mentioned ones, we have a total of 135 cases with no interruptions. Compared to the general trigram pattern (XXX), this gives the following results [χ^2= 3.688, p=.054, d=.322, 99% CI[.947, .953]]. In addition, were also observed structures with fourgrams involving a determiner and a noun between the verb and its particle (VB DT NN RP). Among the nine occurrences observed in the corpus, no interruptions were observed. A recapitulation of the structures involving a verb and a particle is provided in table 2.

Structure	IR	# cases	Structure	IR	# cases
VB RP	0	534	Miscellaneous VB X RP	0	21
VB RP IN	0	45	VB DT NN RP	0	9
VB PPO RP	0	51	Total VB X RP	0	135
VB PRON RP	0	18			

Table 2 Recapitulation of the structures involving a verb and a particle

3.4 Verb's indirect objects

Some verbs in English require a preposition to introduce their object complement, called the *indirect object*. In the linguistic literature, the preposition introducing the object is processed in different ways. On the one hand, Phrase Structure Grammar (PSG) considers this preposition as a part of a complex unit, called Prepositional Phrase (PP), made of the preposition and a noun phrase. As such complex units are not allowed within the chunking framework proposed by (Abney, 1994), here, on the other hand, the preposition is given a standalone status, where it is considered to form its own chunk. Given the strong semantic correlation between the verb and its preposition, many foreign language manuals and dictionaries provide the verbs with their preposition like *depends on* and *depends to*. In this third case, the preposition has a privileged relation with the verb rather than with the noun. The IR of the bigrams (VB IN) and (IN NN) are respectively .005 and .015. This difference in frequency turns out to be statistically significant [χ^2=6.977, p=.0083, d=.101, 99% CI[.973, .995]]. Furthermore, the IR of the bigram (IN VB) is .018, which is larger than the IR of the bigram (VB IN). This difference is also statistically significant [χ^2= 9.632, p=.001, d=.103, 99% CI[.972, .990]]. This suggests that the verb is more connected with the preposition as its argument than being the argument of a preposition.

4 Discussion

4.1 Disfluencies and utterance syntactic complexity

The first question raised in this paper was whether the syntactic complexity increase yields an increase in the number of disfluencies. The reported results in table 1 confirmed this hypothesis. The correlations with the five considered measures were all positive and statistically significant. This confirms the general conception about disfluency as being caused by a heavy cognitive processing related to the task or to the linguistic complexity. For example, (Cook *et al.*, 1974) have shown that the rate of filled pauses increased with the increase of a complexity measured by the length of the following clause (no significant results were found with the subordination index devised by Frieda Goldman-Eiseler). This was also confirmed by Ferreira's work (Ferreira, 1991). A more recent work based on corpus study also shown that disfluencies occurrences correlate with the macro syntax and discourse (Beliao and Lacheret, 2013).

4.2 Verb, particle, and the planning of the complements

Given the strong relationship between the verb and its particle, this latter may be considered as a separate morpheme of the verb. Hence, an easy interpretation of the null IR between the verb and the particle in the bigram (VB RP) is to consider that this is happening because of a morphological reason; no syntax is involved here. However, similar, statistically significant, patterns were also observed with the trigram (VB X RP), where X may be any category among 11 possible complements of the verb. Although the data were not large enough to achieve significance with fourgrams, the zero IR was observed in this case as well. This is a clear indication that syntax is behind this phenomenon as it is not possible to imagine a morphological relationship between the verb and such a diverse group of categories. Put within a larger perspective, this confirms the idea that syntax is deeply embedded within the planning process of spoken language production.

4.3 Verb, its subject and object

Given the linearity of human language, it is widely thought today that language production is an incremental process. However, there are several models of incrementality that diverge in their fundamental stipulations of the timing of conceptual encoding and the timing of grammatical structures' creation. Some believe that this process is done in a "word-by-word" fashion and therefore it is completely linear (Branigan, 2008), (Kempen and Hoenkamp 1987). In other words, according to this model, during piecemeal formulation of utterances, verbs are planned only briefly before they are uttered. On the other hand, hierarchical incrementality assumes that, at the beginning of the utterance generation, its "linguistic blueprint" is formulated (Kuchinsky et al., 2011), (Zenzi and Bock, 2000). According to a lighter version of hierarchical incrementality, planning begins with the thematic structure of the event, where the relation between the agent and the patient is encoded (Bock et al, 2004). Finally, Ferreira's model of language production, which is based on Tree Adjoining Grammar, stipulates that the lexical selection of the verb is necessary before the speaker can plan the subject (Ferreira, 2000).

The data in section 3.2 show that the verb is more connected to its subject than to its object. This supports a light hierarchical incremental planning. A *verb-first* approach, such as the one proposed by (Ferreira, 2000), entails that we should not see interruptions between the verb and the subject. On the other hand, a linear incrementality would lead to equal interruption rates between the verb and its subject and its object.

4.4 Verb, particle, and preposition

The results presented in section 3.3 confirm the common conception in the classic grammar according to which particles are more tightly related to verbs than to prepositions. They also suggest, nevertheless, that prepositions have a privileged relationship with the verbs they complement. On the other hand, when the preposition is located before the verb, its IR with the verb is much larger than when it is after. This suggests that the nature of its relationship with the verb is different in this case. A possible reason is that the preposition is introducing a new proposition (via the verb) making it an important articulation point inside the sentence. One could ask if this is simply due to the prosodic structure of the utterance rather than the syntactic one.

Numerous previous studies have shown that pitch, accents, and intonation have a strong correlation with the sentence's syntactic structure (Nespor and Vogel, 2007), (Inkelas and Zec, 1990). Although several studies have attempted to use dependency grammar as a descriptive framework for prosody-syntax congruence (Mertens, 2009), (Gerdes, Hi-Yon, 2003), the majority of the existing linguistic and psycholinguistic models are based on phrase structure approaches to syntax. For example, (Cooper and Paccia-Cooper, 1980) proposed a model based on the idea that the likelihood of an intonational boundary correlates with the increase of the number of syntactic brackets at a word boundary. Hence, the likelihood of a boundary at the ends of syntactic constituents occurs more than at the beginning. Also, Ferreira (1988) proposed a model based on X-bar theory where syntax and semantics play a role in intonational phrasing. According to Ferreira this increases the semantic coherence as it minimizes the number of dependencies across units. As we saw, the patterns (VB IN) and (IN VB) have equal prosodic status (both are located at phrase borders) but different IR. This confirms that the difference is related to the nature of the syntactic relation.

5 Conclusion

This paper is about a corpus study of the interruption by simple disfluencies between key components of the utterance. The basic assumption behind this study is that interruptions depend on syntactic factors. The results confirmed some well-known facts about English syntax such as the tight interrelation between the verb and the particle. Furthermore, it also has shown a tight relation between the verb and its preposition compared to the relation between the preposition and the subsequent NP. Also, the tight relation between the verb and its subject supports the conception of light hierarchical incremental planning of language production. Beyond the direct facts, this work offers a quantitative description of the cognitive dependencies between the words with probability-like scores.

Different paths are worth to explore after this work. One of them is to study similar phenomena in language acquisition corpora. This could give us interesting insights about whether these patterns are innate or if they evolve throughout time. Covering more types of disfluencies can also bring insights about possible differences between the patterns involving each type. Finally, using a larger corpus such as the Switchboard Corpus could help confirm the obtained figures.

6 Acknowledgement

I gratefully acknowledge the helpful feedback of Professor Joseph A. Durlak on the interpretation of the statistical results.

7 Bibliography

Steven Abney. 1994. Parsing by chunks. Bell Communication Research. November 10. http://www.vinartus.net/spa/90e.pdf

Julie Beliao and Lacheret Anne. 2013. Disfluency and discursive markers: when prosody and syntax plan discourse, DiSS 2013: The 6th Workshop on Disfluency in Spontaneous Speech, Aug, Stockholm, Sweden. 54 (1), pp.5-9, 201.

K. Bock, and Levelt W.J.M. 1994. Language production. Grammatical encoding. IN M.A. Gernsbacher (Ed.). Handbook of psycholinguistics (pp.741-779). New York: Academic Press.

K. Bock, D. E Irwin and D. J. Davidson. 2004. Putting first things first. In J. M. Henderson, & F. Ferreira (Eds.), The interface of language, vision, and action: What we can learn from free-viewing eye tracking (pp. 249–278). New York: Psychology Press.

D. S. Boomer. 1965. Hesitation and grammar encoding. language and speech, Vol 8, Issue 3.

H. P. Branigan. M. J. Pickering, M. N. Tanaka. 2008. Contributions of animacy to grammatical function assignment and word order during production. Lingua 118, 172–189.

J. G. Carbonell and P.J HAYES. 1984. Recovery strategies for parsing extragrammatical language. American Journal of Computational linguistics. 9(3-4), pp123-146.

M. Cook, J. Smith and Lalljee, M. 1974. Filled pauses and syntactic complexity. Language and Speech. 17, 11-16.

Mark G. Core. 1999. Dialog parsing: from speech repairs to speech acts. Ph.D. dissertation, University of Rochester, New York.

William E. Cooper, Jeanne Paccia-Cooper. 1980. Syntax and Speech. Harvard University Press. ISBN 9780674283947.

G.S. Dell, Change, F., and Griffin, Z.M. (1999). Connectionist models of language production: lexical access and grammatical encoding. Cognitive Review. 23:517-542.

Fernanda Ferreira. 1988. Planning and timing in sentence production: The syntax-to-phonology conversion. Unpublished dissertation, University of Massachusetts, Amherst, MA.

Fernanda Ferreira. 2000. Syntax in language production: An approach using tree-adjoining grammars. In L. Wheeldon (Ed.), Aspects of language production (pp. 291–330). London: Psychology Press.

Fernanda Ferreira. 1991. Effects of length and syntactic complexity on initiation times for prepared utterances, Journal of Memory and Language, 30: 210-233.

Fernanda Ferreira. 2000. Syntax in language production: An approach using Tree-Adjoining Grammars. In L. Wheeldon (Ed.), Aspects of language production. Cambridge, MA: MIT Press.

Marilyn Ford and Virginia M. Holmes. 1978. Planning units and syntax in sentence production. Cognition Volume 6, Issue 1, March. Pages 35-53.

V. A. Fromkin. 1973. Speech Errors as Linguistic Evidence. The Hague, Netherlands: Mouton.

M.F. Garrett. 1980. The limits of accommodation. In V. Fromkin (Ed.), Errors in linguistic performance. (pp. 263-271). New York: Academic.

M.F. Garrett. 1988. Processes in language production. in F. J. NEWMEYER (editor), Linguistics: the Cambridge Survey, Vol. III: language: psychological and biological aspects, Cambridge: Cambridge University Press.

Kim Gerdes and Yoo Hi-Yon. 2003.The fields on the way to prosody Alternatives to phrase structure based approaches to prosody. ICPhS Barcelona, Spain, August 3-9.

A. Pearl Gordon, L. Harold Luper. 1989. Speech disfluencies in nonstutterers: Syntactic complexity and production task effects, Journal of Fluency Disorders, Volume 14, Issue 6, December Pages 429-445.

Robert Hartsuiker and Kolk Herman. 2001. Error Monitoring in Speech Production: A Computational Test of the Perceptual Loop Theory. Cognitive Psychology 42(2):113-57 April.

WO Haynes and SB Hood. 1978. Disfluency changes in children as a function of the systematic modification of linguistic complexity. Journal of Communication Disorders 1978 Feb;11(1):79-93.

Peter Heeman and James Allen. 1995. The trains 93 dialogs, TRAINS Technical note94-2, The University of Rochester computer science department, March.

Peter Heeman and James Allen. 1999. Speech repairs, intonational phrases, and discourse markers: modeling speakers' utterances in spoken dialogue, Computational Linguistics 25 (4), 527-571.

Sharon Inkelas and Draga Zec, (editors). 1990. The Phonology-Syntax Connection, The University of Chicago Press. ISBN 0226381013.

G. Kempen E. Hoenkamp. 1987. An incremental procedural grammar for sentence formulation. Cognitive Science, Volume 11, Issue 2, April, 1987 https://doi.org/10.1207/s15516709cog1102_5

Kirsten Malmkjaer. 2002. The linguistics encyclopedia, Second Edition, London/New York, Routledge.

Stefanie Kuchinsky K. Bock D. E. Irwin. 2011. Reversing the hands of time: changing the mapping from seeing to saying. Journal of Experimental Psychology: Learning, Memory, and Cognition, Vol 37(3), May 2011, 748-756.

M. Zakaria Kurdi. 2016. Natural language processing and computational linguistics 1: speech, morphology and syntax. John Wiley & Sons, ISBN-10: 1848218486.

M. Zakaria Kurdi. 2002. Combining pattern matching and shallow parsing techniques for detecting and correcting spoken language extragrammaticalities. 2nd Workshop on RObust Methods in Analysis of Natural Language Data ROMAND 2002, Frascati-Rome, Italy - July 17.

M. Zakaria Kurdi. 2003. Contribution à l'analyse du langage oral spontané, Ph.D dissertation, Joseph Fourier University, Grenoble, France.

M. Zakaria, Kurdi. 2017. Lexical and Syntactic Features Selection for an Adaptive Reading Recommendation System Based on Text Complexity. Proceedings of the 2017 International Conference on Information System and Data Mining, Charleston, SC, USA — April 01 - 03, 2017, pages 66-69.

W. J. M. Levelt, A. Roelofs, and Meyer, A. S. 1999. A theory of lexical access in speech production. Behavioral and Brain Sciences. 22(1), 1–75.

W.J. M. Levelt. 1983. Monitoring and self-repair in speech. Cognition 14, 41-104.

Anders Lindström, Jessica Villing, Staffan Larsson, Er Seward, Cecilia Holtelius and Ab Veridict. 2008. The effect of cognitive load on disfluencies during in-vehicle spoken dialogue, In Proceedings of the 9th Annual Conference of the International Speech Communication Association (INTERSPEECH 2008), 22-26 September, Brisbane, Australia.

Kenneth Logan K., L. LaSalle. 1999. Grammatical characteristics of children's conversational utterances that contain disfluency clusters. Journal of Speech, Language, and Hearing Research, vol. 42, pp. 80–91, Feb.

Scott F. McLaughlin Walter L. Cullinan. 1989. Disfluencies, utterance length, and linguistic complexity in nonstuttering children, Journal of Fluency Disorders, Volume 14, Issue 1, February, Pages 17-36.

Marie W Meteer Ann A Taylor et al, 1995. Dysfluency annotation stylebook for the Switchboard corpus, M. Meteer and A. Taylor. Disfluency annotation stylebook for the Switchboard corpus. Department of Computer and Information Science, University of Pennsylvania. ftp://ftp.cis.upenn.edu/pub/treebank/swbd/doc/DFL-book.ps. Accessed 2018.

M. Nespor, I. Vogel. 2007. Prosodic Phonology. Berlin-New York, Mouton de Gruyter. ISBN 3110197901.

N. Nozari, G.S. Dell, M.F. Schwartz. 2011. Is comprehension the basis for error detection? A conflict-based theory of error detection in speech production. Cognitive Psychology, 63(1), 1-33.

Piet Mertens, Prosodie, syntaxe et discours : autour d'une approche prédictive, In Yoo, H-Y & Delais-Roussarie, E. (eds), proceedings d'IDP, Paris, Septembre 2009, ISSN 2114-7612, pp. 19-32, 2009.

Ralph Rose. 2017. Silent and filled pauses and speech planning in first and second language production. In Eklund, R. and Rose, R. (Eds.), Proceedings of DiSS 2017, Disfluency in Spontaneous Speech. Stockholm, Sweden: Royal Institute of Technology (KTH), ISSN 1104-5787, pp. 49-52.

Michael Wagner. 2016. Information Structure and Production Planning. In Caroline Fery and Shin Ishihara editors, Oxford Handbook on Information Structure. Oxford University Press, Oxford.

M. Griffin Zenzi and Kathryn Bock. 2000. What the Eyes Say About Speaking. Psychological Science Vol 11, Issue 4, 2000, 274-279.

Word-word Relations in Dementia and Typical Aging

Natalia Arias-Trejo and **Aline Minto-García** and **Diana I. Luna-Umanzor**
and **Alma E. Ríos-Ponce** and **Gemma Bel-Enguix** and **Mariana Balderas-Pliego**
Universidad Nacional Autónoma de México
04510 Ciudad de México, CDMX
`enariast@unam.mx, amintog@hotmail.com`
`diana.luna.umzr@hotmail.com, ariosponce@gmail.com`
`gbele@iingen.unam.mx, balderaspmn@gmail.com`

Abstract

sssss Older adults tend to suffer a decline in some of their cognitive capabilities, being language one of least affected processes. Word association norms (WAN) also known as free word associations reflect word-word relations, the participant reads or hears a word and is asked to write or say the first word that comes to mind. Free word associations show how the organization of semantic memory remains almost unchanged with age. We have performed a WAN task with very small samples of older adults with Alzheimer's disease (AD), vascular dementia (VaD) and mixed dementia (MxD), and also with a control group of typical aging adults, matched by age, sex and education. All of them are native speakers of Mexican Spanish. The results show, as expected, that Alzheimer disease has a very important impact in lexical retrieval, unlike vascular and mixed dementia. This suggests that linguistic tests elaborated from WAN can be also used for detecting AD at early stages.

1 Introduction

According to the World Health Organization (2015), aging is a process associated with molecular and cellular damage, which leads to a general decline of the person and, eventually, its death. Among the changes caused by age, some degree of cognitive decline is commonly observed in older adults, and the proportion of elderly people who suffer this decline increases (Rog and Fink, 2013). This decline has been measured through neuropsychological evaluations, which have shown two common profiles in elderly people, those who present successful aging, meaning a proper execution in cognitive tasks, as well as in daily life, and those who present cognitive impairment (Ardila and Rosselli, 2007) or neurocognitive disorders according to the DSM-5 (American Psychiatric Association, 2013).

As mentioned before, aging causes a general decline in elderly people, which can be observed at anatomical and physiological levels and it is intimately linked to cognitive and emotional changes (Cummings and Benson, 1992). During senescence, a decrease in memory capacity and learning is representative of the cognitive profile exhibited, showing a pattern in which forgetfulness rate increases within the fifth decade of life, while their learning ability is decreased, characteristics that will progress slowly through time and will give us cues of pathology, especially in people with dementia, where this process will be particularly accelerated (Ardila and Rosselli, 2007).

Elderly people show more alterations in episodic memory than semantic memory, especially when the memories need more effort to be remembered (consciousness) than those performed automatically and based in familiarity. In addition, it is also known that age affects the process of codification, especially when strategic thinking is needed, and the recovery process, where the use of cues is required to recall information. Finally, it is common that elderly people show problems in context memories, meaning the context in which an event was developed, rather than content memory, meaning the memory of the event, while prospective memory, meaning the ability to remember future events (e.g., remember to do something or going somewhere), also is affected due to a lack of accessibility to internal cues and auto initiated processes (Jurado et al., 2013).

On the contrary, the least affected cognitive process by aging is language, a process that has shown improvement throughout life, especially in items such as vocabulary. Nonetheless, this process can be

Proceedings of the First International Workshop on Language Cognition and Computational Models, pages 85–93
Santa Fe, New Mexico, United States, August 20, 2018.
https://doi.org/10.18653/v1/P17

affected by other elements of cognition, such as memory, which can cause phonologic recovery of words, provoking anomia commonly known as "tip of the tongue phenomenon" (Jurado et al., 2013).

The problem is very relevant for linguists, because approaching the different types of anomias caused by illness can help to describe how words are connected in the lexicon. Moreover, there is a lack of description of the specific language difficulties associated with different illnesses and their stages. To do that, we propose a Word Association Norms (WAN, from here) approach, that understands lexicon as linked data, being the change in the of the links the best way to explain the cognitive deterioration. Having more information about this would help linguists and cognitive scientists to model a theory of memory.

The present research aims to investigate the type of semantic relationships generated by seven patients with dementia and their typically aging peers, matched by sex, age and years of education.

From here, our paper is structured as follows. Section 2 introduces a psychological description of the types of dementia that we are approaching. Section 3 some basic ideas on Word Association Norms are provided, as well as their relevance for linguistics, psychology and computer science. In 4, we explain the experiment, whose results are presented at 5. We finish the paper with the discussion and future work perspectives at 6.

2   Alzheimer's Disease, Vascular Dementia and Mixed Dementia

The information obtained about the cognition and lifestyle in elderly people has shown great importance in the establishment of criteria to diagnose neurocognitive disorders such as dementias- and their origin, as cognition has specific variations according to the origin of each disorder. In pathological aging the severity of an impairment, both physical and cognitive, can interfere in various ways in the family, social and occupational functioning of the subject. The most serious level of pathological aging is known as dementia (Portellano, 2005). Dementia is a syndrome due to a brain disease, usually of chronic or progressive nature, which can alter multiple superior cortical functions, also, all alterations in cognitive function are accompanied by a deterioration of emotional or social control, as well as behavior or motivation (Jurado et al., 2013). All types of dementia involve mental decline that (Alzheimer's Association, 2006):

- occurred from a higher level (for example, the person didn't always have a poor memory)

- is severe enough to interfere with usual activities and daily life

- affects more than one of the following four core mental abilities

    - recent memory (the ability to learn and recall new information)
    - language (the ability to write or speak, or to understand written or spoken words)
    - visuospatial function (the ability to understand and use symbols, maps, etc., and the brains ability to translate visual signals into a correct impression of where objects are in space)
    - executive function (the ability to plan, reason, solve problems and focus on a task)

Alzheimer's disease (AD) and vascular dementia (VaD) are the two most common forms of dementia (Formiga et al., 2008). AD is characterized by the formation of plaques of the amyloid beta protein which produces neuronal death (Quiroz Baez, 2010). In VaD, various cognitive alterations are caused by cerebrovascular diseases (Portellano, 2005). Mixed dementia (MxD), for example, is believed to be caused by Alzheimer's disease in combination with some cerebral vascular disease; it represents between 13 and 17% of cases worldwide (Cervantes et al., 2017).

At present, our society experiences an increase in the numbers of years that people live. Although many benefits, this increase also implies an increase in physical illnesses and cognitive deterioration. Dementia is one of the illnesses that increases its presence as people get older. One of the areas that is frequently affected is language. Language problems in dementia tend to be detected when they are notorious. By that time, there is very little that can be studied or even ameliorated. Thus, it is essential to evaluate language skills at the early stages of dementia or at least as early as it is diagnosed.

3   Word Association Norms

Word association (WA) tests are an experimental technique for discovering the way that human minds structure knowledge (De Deyne et al., 2013). In a free word association experiment, the participant reads or hears a word (*stimulus*) and is asked to write or say the first word that comes to mind (*response*) (Hirsh and Tree, 2001). Free WA tests are able to produce rich types of associations that can reflect both semantic and episodic memory contents (Borge-Holthoefer and Arenas, 2009).

Word Association Norms (WAN) are collections of WA taken in different populations. From these collections some measures can be studied. The most frequent word provided as the output of a given input word is considered as being the first associate (FA). The strength of association of the first associate, that in the paper is referred as AS, represents the proportion of participants who responded with the same first associate. This, among other measures, such as total of associates (number of different answers given), idiosyncratic answers (answers given by only one participant in the whole sample), blank answers (words to which the participant didn't give any answer in the established period of time) are calculated to understand how connected a lexical network is for a group of participants with similar background (Callejas et al., 2003; Salles et al., 2008).

From the many experiments performed in many languages, it has been concluded that there is uniformity in the organization of associations and people shared stable networks of connections among words (Istifci, 2010).

We performed a Word Association Norms (WANs) task, also known as free word association task. WANs are generally taken in young healthy adults, generally, university students. Comparisons between young and old adults have increased our understanding about the potential effects of aging on deficits in the lexical network. Generally speaking, comparisons between WANs produced by young and old adults allow us to conclude that there is very little change in the organisation of semantic memory with age, at least in word associations (Burke and Peters, 1986; Tresselt and Maizner, 1964). It has been found that in old adults, the connections in the semantic network are abundant and resistant to deficits (D.G. MacKay, 2001). For example, an overlap of 60.5% in the three most frequent responses between young and old adults was reported by Burke and Peters (1986). Moreover, these authors retested 2 to 3 months later part of their study with a subsample from the original and found that both, young and old adults were consistent in providing the same first associate for word pairs with a high strength of association than with low strength of association, arguing that old adults do not seem to have a retrieval problem as they were generating in an automatic fashion their responses which were stored in semantic memory. Hirsh and Tree (2001) also reported an overlap of 60% between the top three responses of a group of British young and old adults.

In contrast, research has reported changes in the semantic network exhibited by adults with neurological diseases. Kent and Rosanoff (1910) tested 100 words with the participation of 1000 normal subjects as well as 247 participants with a mental disease dementia praecox, paranoic conditions, manic-depressive states, epilepsy, among others finding some tendencies about a gradual, but not an abrupt change from a normal mental state to a pathological one.

Borge-Holthoefer and Arenas (2009) established a relation between cognitive illness and the capability to walk the graph or our semantic relations. This difficulty could come from the degradation of the graph, this is the weakening of the links between the words. Following this hypothesis, it is a key aspect of the research to establish the weight of the regular connections in contrast with the ones showed by patients with dementia.

According to Clark (1970), the rules of relationship words from free association are based on syntagmatic and paradigmatic relations. Through this traditional classification, paradigmatic responses belong to the same grammatical class of the stimulus words and they are generally similar words in conceptual terms because they share some semantic features (e. g., dog-cat, white-black, eat-drink). While syntagmatic responses belong to a different grammatical category of the stimulus words, which might appear next in the same sentence (e. g., house-large, high-giraffe, walk-slowly). Thus, older adult speakers of English show greater variability in word association unlike young adults, also it has been found that they tend to provide a greater amount of paradigmatic responses (Burke and Peters, 1986; Lovelance and

Cooley, 1982). In contrast to these findings, research with German has reported a decrease in the emergence of paradigmatic responses (K. Riegel and R. M. Riegel, 1964). Most researches focused on this population concluded that a dominant emergence of paradigmatic responses in word association tasks exists.

Changes in the predominance of paradigmatic or syntagmatic responses are observed in dementia. Gewirth et al. (1984) reported that participants with dementia or aphasics tended to provide paradigmatic responses for nouns and adjectives and syntagmatic for verbs and adverbs. Although the mechanism producing syntagmatic responses were similar to normal patients, paradigmatic responses were less efficient in dementia and more random producing then more idiosyncratic responses. Also, dementia patients tended, more than aphasic or normal adults, to perseverate responses. Eustache et al. (1990) showed that as the severity of dementia increased, AD patients were less likely to give a frequent response. Recently, Preethi and Goswani (2016) showed reduced levels in the first association strength in a word association task of participants either with dementia or aphasia, but not in neuro-typical participants. Interestingly, paradigmatic responses were significantly more affected than the syntagmatic ones. Gollan et al. (2006), as in Gewirth et al.s study, also reported a semantic deficit in AD patients depending on the type of word. Differences between controls and AD patients were found for strong associated stimuli (e.g., bride-groom), but not for weak stimuli (e.g., bride-pretty): AD participants generated less common responses for the strong, but not the weak stimuli. Gollan et al. argued that weak associations are less semantic, and thus less dependent on meaning.

At present, little is known regarding the potential differences in a semantic deficit that may be encountered in AD patients as opposed to other dementias. The current work aimed to compare Alzheimer, mixed and vascular dementia.

4 Method

4.1 Participants

In this study 14 elder adults participated. Half of the participants had dementia and the other half was the control or healthy- aging group. Dementia group included participants with Alzheimer's disease (n = 2) phase one and two, Vascular (n = 3) and Mixed Dementia (n = 2). All of them had previously received the diagnosis from their physicians. The group consisted in 3 men and 4 women, its mean age was 78.29 years age span was 67 to 85 years old, and the education average 9.28 years. The healthy-aging group no neurological diseases was formed equivalent as possible in sex, age and years of education to the Dementia group. Its mean age was 78.14 years (age span 67 to 85 years old) and the average years of schooling was 9.33 years.

It is important to emphasize that participants selected for the sample were only those whose dementia progression did not show impairment in most of their daily life basic skills (e.g. toileting or feeding) according to their physicians and caregivers. It was also taken into consideration their ability or willingness to finish the word association task, causing a significant reduction of the sample. However, as they were paired with controls through age, gender and educational degree criteria and exclusively compared with the group that constituted their paired controls, this work can be taken into account as a case-control study, until more participants can be included to generalize results.

Although our sample does not permit the generalization of the results, it allows researchers to have an insight about the language changes that take place as a result of each type of dementia and effect of other variables. However, in the case of vascular dementia results (such as lack of FA) can be determined by the cause or the region affected by the cerebrovascular accident, having a different effect on cognition that should be taken into account in future studies with a sample that can allow dividing participants in subgroups.

4.2 Procedure

Participants performed a free-word association task in which 120 familiar and frequent words in Spanish were orally presented, one-by-one, by an experimenter who manipulated the laptop in which an application presented the input words in a previously set-up order. The experimenter wrote in a computer the participants answers. If after 30 seconds, the participant remained in silence, the experimenter who received an automatic visual notification after 30 seconds repeated orally once more the input word. If after another 30 seconds, the patient did not produce an answer, the system automatically exhibited the following word. If the participant did not produce an answer for three consecutive input words, the experimenter repeated the instructions and continue with the task.

4.3 Data analysis

The application stored the answers written by the experimenter for further analyses. Initially, two experimenters edited the data so that there were no language errors in the answers, for example, orthographical mistakes. The experimenters also unified the responses using a lemmatization process. In Spanish a contrast between masculine and feminine exists, where some words in feminine tend to end in a and in masculine in o. Thus, the answers were unified to the masculine ending (niño, niña was unified to niño). In the same way, every verbal form has been unified to the infinitive.

Later, an analysis of the lexical relation between every *stimulus* and its FA was carried out. Every pair was labelled as a paradigmatic or syntagmatic relation, following the definition given by (Clark, 1970).

5 Results

An analysis with some of the conventional measures reported in word association norms was performed, including the association strength of the first associate (AS), number of blank answers (BA), and mean response time (RT) taken to provide the first associate.

For every *stimulus* the values AF and RF are calculated. AF, *absolute frequency* refers to the absolute frequency of syntagmatic and paradigmatic responses. RF, *relative frequency*, retrieves the percentage relation between syntagmatic and paradigmatic responses.

The AS, *association strength* of the FA, first associate, to every stimulus has also been obtained, with the following formula: being N the total number of answers in the sample for a stimulus word, and F the frequency of a given response

$$AS = \frac{F * 100}{N}$$

With the aim of evaluating if the means AS (association strength of the first associate), BA (blank responses), and RT (response time) provided by each of the three experimental groups (AD, MxD and VaD) were significantly different to their control groups, we performed a series of comparisons.

With the aim of evaluating if the means AS (association strength of first associate), BA (blank responses), and RT (response time) provided by each of the three experimental groups (AD, MxD and Vad) were significantly different to their control groups, we performed a series of mean comparisons.

5.1 Statistical Results

Each type of dementia was compared with their control group through t-tests for independent measures. In the comparison between the group diagnosed with AD and their respective controls for AS significant differences were observed between both groups ($t(234) = -4.17$; $p < 0.005$), where the group with AD presented less strength in their FA (0.08 ± 0.4) than the control group (0.44 ± 0.83). Also, the comparison between MxD and their control group for the AS of the FA showed significant differences between both groups ($t(234) = -3.34$; $p = 0.001$), where the control group presented a higher associate strength (0.76 ± 1.05) than the group with MxD (0.35 ± 0.8). Finally, the group diagnosed with VaD did not provide a common FA because the responses as FA were different, thus their association strength was null. This lack of associate strength is significantly different when compared with their control group ($t(234) = -4.589118$; $p < 0.005$), where the control group did present common first associates (0.3 ± 0.72). For blank answers (BA), significant differences between the AD and the control group were encountered ($t(234) = 14.02$; $p < 0.005$), where the AD group presented blank answers (0.62 ± 0.48) but the control group didn't. Non-significant differences were found between MxD and controls ($t(234) = 0.85$; $p = 0.39$), where MxD presented a slightly higher number of BA (0.06 ± 0.25) than the control group (0.04 ± 0.20). Both, the VaD and controls showed a lack of BA. Finally, in the case of reaction times

	AS	BA	RT
AD	0.08± 0.4	0.62± 0.48	11.57± 8.22
CG	0.44± 0.83	0	5.92± 2.79
MxD	0.35± 0.8	0.06± 0.25	4.67± 2.27
CG	0.76± 1.05	0.04 ± 0.20	5.57± 2.23
VaD	N.D.	N.D.	4.96± 2.1
CG	0.3± 0.72	N.D.	4.51± 1.69

Table 1: Comparative strength between AD, MxD, VaD and their respective control groups in AS, BA and RF.

	AS		BA		RT	
	$t(234)$	p	$t(234)$	p	$t(234)$	p
AD vs CG	-4.17	< 0.005	14.02	<0.005	7.05	<0.005
MxD vs CG	-3.34	0.001	0.85	0.39	-3.08	0.0023
VaD vs CG	-4.58	<0.005	N.D.	N.D.	1.77	0.07

Table 2: t-tests performed comparing AD, MxD, VaD and their respective control groups in AS, BA and RF.

(RT), significant differences between the AD group and their controls were observed ($t(234) = 7.05$; $p < 0.005$), where the AD group took more time to give an answer (11.57 ± 8.22) than the control group (5.92 ± 2.79). Similar results were found between MxD and controls ($t(234) = -3.08$; $p = 0.0023$), where the group with MxD took more time to elicit a response (4.675706 ± 2.271421) than the control group (5.57 ± 2.23). Conversely, non-significant differences were encountered between the VaD and control groups ($t(234) = 1.77$; $p = 0.07$), RT for the VaD group (4.96 ± 2.1) and their control group (4.51 ± 1.69). Tables 1 and 2 can help to visualize the results.

To determine differences between dementia groups, an univariate ANOVA was done with groups AD, MxD and VaD as factors. This ANOVA determined statistically significant differences for AS between groups ($F(2) = 15.199$, $p < 0.05$). Post-hoc tests using Bonferroni corrections showed that the MxD group AS was higher ($M = 0.35$, $SD = 0.8$) than that for the AD group (M=0.0847, SD=0.40459) and VaD group (no AS generated). Meanwhile for BA, the univariate ANOVA showed significant differences ($F(2) = 139.970$, $p < 0.05$) between AD and the other groups, where AD had more BA ($M = 0.62$, $SD = 0.48$) than MxD ($M = 0.06$, $SD = 0.25$) and VaD (no BA were provided). Finally, the ANOVA for RT showed statistically significant differences ($F(2) = 69.737$, $p < 0.05$) where Bonferroni correction showed that AD group had a slower reaction time ($M = 11.57$, $SD = 8.22$) than MxD ($M = 4.67$, $SD = 2.27$) and VaD ($M = 4.96$, $SD = 2.1$).

5.2 Syntagmatic and Paradigmatic relations

With the responses provided by the participants (94.8%) a classification according to the type of relationship between the stimulus and its response was carried out. The classification took into account syntagmatic and paradigmatic relations (Clark, 1970), as well as unclassifiable responses (e. g., idiosyncratic responses or onomatopoeias). Overall, the participants showed a higher proportion of paradigmatic responses (51.63%), followed by the syntagmatic responses and unclassifiable responses (47.42% and 0.94%, respectively). Table 5.2 presents the Absolute frequency (AF) and Relative frequency (RF) for both paradigmatic and syntagmatic responses. AF refers to the total number of responses and RF to the proportion (calculated by dividing the AF by the total number of cases) from participants with AD, MxD, VaD, and their respective control groups.

The AD group and control group differed in the proportion of paradigmatic and syntagmatic responses

	Paradigmatic		Syntagmatic		Unclassifiable	
	AF	RF	AF	RF	AF	RF
AD	51	30.91	107	64.85	7	4.24
CG	148	61.67	89	37.08	3	1.25
MxD	197	55.81	156	44.19	0	0.00
CG	181	50.99	173	48.73	1	0.28
VaD	119	49.79	117	48.95	3	1.26
CG	126	52.50	113	47.08	1	0.42

Table 3: Frequency of paradigmatic, syntagmatic and unclassifiable responses per group: AD, MxD, VaD, CG (control group).

generated. Most responses of the AD participants were syntagmatic (64.85%), followed by paradigmatic (30.91%), whereas those in the control group had a higher amount of paradigmatic responses (61.67%), followed by syntagmatic (37.08%). The results showed significant difference between the type of responses for both groups χ^2 (2, N = 4) = 37.95, p = 0.00000001. With respect to older adults with MxD, they showed a discrete higher proportion of paradigmatic responses (55.81%) as the control group (50.99%), syntagmatic responses in both groups were 44.19% and 48.73%, respectively. Non-significant differences were encountered χ^2 (2, N = 6) = 2.55, p = 0.28. Finally, the VaD group and the control group had similar percentages of paradigmatic (49.79% and 52.50%, respectively) and syntagmatic responses. Non-significant differences in paradigmatic responses were found between the two groups (χ^2 (2, N = 4) = 1.26, p = 0.53). As it can be seen, groups of participants with MxD and VaD dementia do not differ from their controls in the type of response provided. However, there are significant differences between groups -AD, VaD, and MxD- in the relationships they established χ^2 (4, N = 7) = 39.50, p = 0.0000001. Those differences are mainly due to contrasts between the AD group and the other two groups MxD and VaD.

6 Discussion

Quantitative results suggest the existence of difficulties to access the lexical semantic memory in participants with dementia, illustrated by the higher quantity of first associates produced by the control group (typically aging group). The difficulties in processes that access lexical memory have been previously studied in typically aging people (Rabadán et al., 1998) and participants with dementia, showing in both groups progressive language problems which onset is present at an early aging-stage (Jaramillo, 2010). We also found differences in the participants' responses according to the type of dementia. The number of AS was higher in MxD compared to AD, while the VaD group showed a lack of associate strength consistent with evidence of greater deficits on semantic memory in this group (Graham et al., 2004).

Similarly, deficits were found when blank answers were analyzed, especially in the groups diagnosed with AD and MxD. This kind of deficits have been previously observed in tasks such as category fluency, confrontational naming task and similarity judgments tasks; therefore, some authors affirm that they are the result of the alteration of semantic memory, which affects the meaning of words, concepts and facts (Jurado et al., 2013).

Furthermore, the increase of reaction times was higher in the groups diagnosed with AD and VaD, which can be related to a decrease in processing speed. Salthouse (1996) and Salthouse et al. (2002) propose that the variance of times observed in almost all cognitive tasks can be explained through the generalized decrease of processing speed. A consequence of the initial decrease in processing speed in complex tasks is to prevent the person to rely on the necessary information to complete the next phase of the task, which could be related to the performance in the task, especially to the number of blank answers produced by the AD and the MxD groups.

Regarding the type of lexical relationships, a greater proportion of paradigmatic responses was observed in both groups of participants with MxD and VaD and their typically-aging peers. Our results follow the same dynamics reported in previous research with neuro-typical older adults. Also, the data of this research agree with the findings about the preference for paradigmatic associations in the population of older adults with typical aging (Lovelance and Cooley, 1982; Burke and Peters, 1986). In contrast to other research (Gewirth et al., 1984; Preethi and Goswani, 2016), the paradigmatic responses of the participants with MxD or VaD were not affected. In this sense, it can be inferred that mixed and vascular dementia do not affect the type of lexical relationships that often predominate in older adults. However, in the case of participants with AD a different phenomenon was observed. Syntagmatic responses were generated in greater proportion, similar to the types of responses provided by young children children younger than 8 years (Ervin, 1961; McNeill, 1970).

The current results indicate that AD causes a change (or regression) in the type of lexical relationships provided by participants. Changes in lexical associations might be taken as a predictor of AD. It seems that, according to this results, a new way for detection of Alzheimer could be developed, based on the types of associations that the patients retrieve. Usually, the strength in the FA is considered to be a good indicator for Alzheimer, but this feature is difficult to test when only one user is compared to a large sample. However, the tendency to provide more syntagmatic than paradigmatic word associations can be a first clue to determine AD. This should be an important line of research to be developed in the future. On the other hand, it would be very interesting to understand how other types of dementia affect word retrieval and the organization of memory. It would be worthwhile to expand the sample to confirm that the presence of these specific conditions does not change the pattern of response.

Aknowledgments

This research was supported by a research grant awarded to Natalia Arias-Trejo by the Mexican Science Council, CONACyT 284731 Normas de Asociacin de Palabras en Pacientes Adultos con Demencia o Enfermedad de Parkinson and PAPIIT Project IA400117 "Simulacin de normas de asociacin de palabras mediante redes de coocurrencias" to Gemma Bel-Enguix. We thank the older adults who participated in the current research.

References

Alzheimer's Association. 2006. Alzheimer's disease and other dementias. Alzheimers Association. Technical report, Alzheimer's Association.

American Psychiatric Association. 2013. Diagnostic and statistical manual of mental disorders (DSM-5). Technical report, American Psychiatric Pub.

A. Ardila and M. Rosselli. 2007. *Neuropsicología clínica*. El Manual Moderno., México.

Javier Borge-Holthoefer and Alex Arenas. 2009. Navigating word association norms to extract semantic information. In *Proceedings of the 31st Annual Conference of the Cognitive Science Society*.

D. Burke and L. Peters. 1986. Word associations in old age: Evidence for consistency in semantic encoding during adulthood. *Psychology and Aging*, 1(4):283–292.

A. Callejas, A. Correa, J. Lupiá nez, and P. Tudela. 2003. Normas asociativas intracategoriales para 612 palabras de seis categorías semánticas en español. *Psicológica*, 24:185–241.

C. Moreno Cervantes, A. Mimenza Alvarado, S. Aguilar Navarro, P. Alvarado Ávila, L. Gutiérrez Gutiérrez, S. Juárez Arellano, and A. Ávila Funes. 2017. Factores asociados a la demencia mixta en comparación con demencia tipo Alzheimer en adultos mayores mexicanos. *Neurología*, 32(5):309–315.

H. Clark. 1970. Word associations and linguistic theory. In *New Horizons in Linguistics*. Penguin, London.

J.L. Cummings and D.F. Benson. 1992. *Dementia: A Clinical Approach*. Butterworths, London.

Simon De Deyne, Daniel J. Navarro, and Gert Storms. 2013. Associative strength and semantic activation in the mental lexicon: Evidence from continued word associations. In *Proceedings of the 35th Annual Conference of the Cognitive Science Society*. Cognitive Science Society.

L.E. James D.G. MacKay. 2001. H. M. Word knowledge and aging: Supports for a new theory of long-term retrograde amnesia. *Psychological Sciences*, 12:485–492.

S. Ervin. 1961. Changes with age in the verbal determinants of word-association. *American Journal of Psychology*, 74:361–372.

F. Eustache, C. Cox, J. Brandt, and L. Pons B. Lechevalier. 1990. Word-association responses and severity of dementia in Alzheimer disease. *Psychological Reports*, 66(3):1315–1322.

F. Formiga, I. Fort, M.J. Robles, D.R. Riu, and O. Sabartes. 2008. Aspectos diferenciales de comorbilidad en pacientes ancianos con demencia tipo Alzheimer o con demencia vascular. *Revista de Neurología*, 46(2):72–76.

L.R. Gewirth, A.G. Shindler, and D.B. Hier. 1984. Altered patterns of word associations in dementia and aphasia. *Brain and Language*, 21(2):307–317.

T.H. Gollan, D.P. Salmon, and J.L. Paxton. 2006. Word association in early Alzheimers disease. *Brain and Language*, 99(3):289–303.

N.L. Graham, T. Emery, and J.R. Hodges. 2004. Distinctive cognitive profiles in Alzheimers disease and subcortical vascular dementia. *Journal of Neurology, Neurosurgery & Psychiatry*, 75:61–71.

K.W. Hirsh and J.J. Tree. 2001. Word association norms for two cohorts of British adults. *Journal of Neurolinguistics*, 14(1):1–44.

Ilknur Istifci. 2010. Playing with words: a study of word association responses. *Journal of International Social Research*, 3(10).

J. Jaramillo. 2010. Demencias: los problemas de lenguaje como hallazgos tempranos. *Acta Neurológica Colombiana*, 26(101-111).

M.A. Jurado, M. Mataró, and R. Pueyo. 2013. *Neuropsicología de las enfermedades neurodegenerativas*. Síntesis, Madrid.

K. Riegel and R. M. Riegel. 1964. Changes in associative behavior during later years of life: A cross-sectional analysis. *Vita Humana*, 7:1–32.

G.H. Kent and A.J. Rosanoff. 1910. A study of association in insanity. *Amer. J. Insanity*, 67(1-2):317–390.

E. Lovelance and S. Cooley. 1982. Free associations of older adults to single words and conceptually related word triads. *Journal of Gerontology*, 37(4):432–437.

D. McNeill. 1970. *The acquisition of language*. Harper & Row, New York.

J.A. Portellano. 2005. Neuropsicología Involutiva. In *Introducción a la Neuropsicología*, pages 314–341. McGraw-Hill, Madrid.

T. Preethi and S.P. Goswani. 2016. Word association ability in persons with aphasia and dementia. *Language in India*, 16(8):134–154.

R. Quiroz Baez. 2010. *Papel del estrs oxidativo en el metabolismo > amiloidognico y toxicidad de la protena B-amiloide. Implicaciones en la > enfermedad de Alzheimer*. Ph.D. Thesis, UNAM, Mexico.

O.J. Rabadán, M.R.E. De Juan, A. P. Rozas, and M. Torres. 1998. Problemas de acceso léxico en la vejez. Bases para la intervención. *Anales de psicología*, 14(2):169.

L.A. Rog and J.W. Fink. 2013. Mild Cognitive Impairment and Normal Aging. In *Handbook on the Neuropsychology of Aging and Dementia*, pages 239–260. Springer.

J.F. Salles, C. Steffen Holderbaum, N. Becker, J. Carvalho Rodrigues, F. Veiga Liedtke, M.R. Zibetti, and L. Ferreira Piccoli. 2008. Normas de associação semântica para 88 palavras do português brasileiro. *Psico*, 39(3):362–2370.

T. Salthouse, D.E. Berish, and J.D. Miles. 2002. The role of cognitive stimulation on the relations between age and cognitive functioning. *Psychology and Aging*, 17(4):548–557.

T. Salthouse. 1996. The processing-speed theory of adult age differences in cognition. *Psychological Review*, 103(3):403–428.

M.E. Tresselt and M.S. Maizner. 1964. The Kent-Rosanoff word association: Word association norms as a function of age. *Psychon. Sci.*, 1:65–66.

World Health Organization. 2015. World health statistics 2015. Technical report, World Health Organization.

Part-of-Speech Annotation of English-Assamese code-mixed texts: Two Approaches

Ritesh Kumar
Department of Linguistics
K.M. Institute of Hindi and Linguistics
Dr. Bhimrao Ambedkar University, Agra
riteshkrjnu@gmail.com

Manas Jyoti Bora
Department of Linguistics
K.M. Institute of Hindi and Linguistics
Dr. Bhimrao Ambedkar University, Agra
manasjyotimj@gmail.com

Abstract

In this paper, we discuss the development of a part-of-speech tagger for English-Assamese code-mixed texts. We provide a comparison of 2 approaches to annotating code-mixed data a) annotation of the texts from the two languages using monolingual resources from each language and b) annotation of the text through a different resource created specifically for code-mixed data. We present a comparative study of the efforts required in each approach and the final performance of the system. Based on this, we argue that it might be a better approach to develop new technologies using code-mixed data instead of monolingual, 'clean' data, especially for those languages where we do not have significant tools and technologies available till now.

1 Introduction

Code-mixing and code-switching in multilingual societies are two of the most well-studied phenomena within the field of sociolinguistics (Gumperz, 1964; Auer, 1995; Myers-Scotton, 1997; Muysken, 2000; Cardenas-Claros and Isharyanti, 2009). Generally, code-mixing is considered intra-sentential in the sense that it refers to mixing of words, phrases or clauses within the same sentence while code-switching is inter-sentential or even inter-clausal in the sense that one switches to the other language while speaking. In this paper, we will use code-mixing to refer to both these phenomena.

While code-mixing is a very well-studied phenomena within the field of theoretical linguistics, there have been few works computational modelling of code-mixing. In the past of few years, with the explosion of social media and an urgent need to process the social media data, we have seen quite a few efforts at modelling, automatic identification and processing of code-mixing (most notable among them being (Solorio and Liu, 2008a; Solorio and Liu, 2008b; Nguyen and Dogruoz, 2013; Das and Gambck, 2014; Barman et al., 2014; Vyas et al., 2014) and several others in the two workshops on computational approaches to code-mixing).

In this paper, we discuss the development of a part-of-speech tagger for English-Assamese code-mixed data and also present a comparative study of two different approaches to annotating code-mixed data

a monolingual ensemble approach: reuse the already available tools for individual languages in an ensemble to process the code-mixed data and

b novel multilingual approach: develop new tools exclusively for code-mixed data from the scratch.

It is often argued that it is a much more resource-intensive task to develop separate tools for different kinds of natural language processing of code-mixed data. As such it is desirable to use the pre-existing tools that were developed for different languages for processing code-mixed texts. While this argument holds merit if the languages under consideration have sufficiently large number of tools and applications already available, which may be used. However, this is not the case for a large number of Indian

Proceedings of the First International Workshop on Language Cognition and Computational Models, pages 94–103
Santa Fe, New Mexico, United States, August 20, 2018.
https://doi.org/10.18653/v1/P17

languages, including the major ones. Barring a few exceptions, there is hardly any basic technologies available for most of the Indian languages. In such a situation, developing tools and technologies for code-mixed, multilingual texts might prove to be more efficient and effective than those for monolingual texts. Also, it might be the case that the tools developed for code-mixed texts work better with monolingual texts in comparison to the performance of the tools developed for monolingual texts used with code-mixed texts. In this paper, we discuss the challenges and issues of both the approaches to processing code-mixed data and also discuss the comparative performance of both the approaches and argue for a rather provocative stand - it will be a better and more fruitful idea to develop technologies based on a multilingual, code-mixed data instead of what is considered 'clean', monolingual data not only because code-mixed data will become norm in the near future but also because these technologies might prove to be 'overall' better performing ones of the two.

2 Corpus Collection and Annotation

Since there is no previous corpus available for Assamese-English code-mixed data, we collected a large corpus of such data from four different public Facebook pages:

- https://www.facebook.com/AAZGFC.Official

- https://www.facebook.com/Mr.Rajkumar007

- https://www.facebook.com/ZUBEENsOFFICIAL

- https://www.facebook.com/teenagersofassamm

These facebook pages contain adequate amount of Assamese-English code-mixed data. The dataset was annotated at the word-level with 2 kinds of information language and part-of-speech. These annotations were carried out with an aim to develop two kinds of system

a language identification system, which is needed for annotating the dataset with individual monolingual taggers of the languages in the text and

b part-of-speech tagger for the code-mixed texts.

The annotation schemes are discussed in the following subsections. We also discuss the collection and annotation of monolingual English and Assamese datasets for the experiments.

2.1 Language Annotation of the Dataset

The data was annotated with both the information about the language at the word-level as well as with the part-of-speech tags. The tagset used for the language annotation is given in Table 1.

The data was annotated at 3 levels Matrix Language, Fragment Language and Word-level Code-mixing (WLCM). Matrix language refers to the language of the whole comment and it may be monolingual (Assamese or English), code-mixed (Mix), universal (UNIV) and named entity (NE). If the language is neither of these three, it is annotated as Other - it allows for further annotation of these comments in the dataset with specific language. Fragment language is the word-level annotation of the language and it was annotated with the same set of languages as the matrix language, except Mix. WLCM refers to the phenomenon where the root form of a word is in one language and the affix is in another language. In such cases, the language of the word is annotated as a combination of the two languages which makes up the word. Let us take a look at the following example -

Thik koise..Mission china **Indiar** babey aru A Wondrous Army **Worldr** babey...kiman wait korabo aru..release diok hunkale..

You are right....”Mission China” is **for India** and ”A Wondrous Army” is **for the world**...How long will you make us wait....(You) release immediately..

In this comment, 'Indiar' and 'Worldr' are instances of WLCM, wehere 'India' and 'World' are English words and '-r' is the Assamese marker for benefactive here.

Sl. No.	Top Level	Language	Label
1.	Matrix Languages	1.1, 1.2, 1.3, 1.4, 1.5, 1.6	–
2.	Fragment Languages	1.1, 1.2, 1.4, 1.5, 1.6 pt	–
3.	Word-level Code-mixing	1.7, 1.8, 1.9, 1.10, 1.11, 1.12	–
1.1		Assamese	AS
1.2		English	EN
1.3		Mix	MIX
1.4		Other	OT
1.5		Universal	UNIV
1.6		Named Entity	NE
1.7		Assamese-English	AS-EN
1.8		English-Assamese	EN-AS
1.9		Assamese-Other	AS-OT
1.10		Other-Assamese	OT-AS
1.11		English-Other	EN-OT
1.12		Other-English	OT-EN

Table 1: Language Identification Tagset

2.2 Part-of-Speech Annotation of the Dataset

Universal part-of-speech tags, proposed by the Universal Dependencies was used for annotating the data with part-of-speech information. The tagset is reproduced in Table 2.

In addition to the 17 universal tags included in the Universal Dependencies tagset, 2 tags suffix and prefix - were included in the tagset. It was necessitated by the kind of data that we encountered in our dataset. There were several instances where the affixes in the Assamese text (written in Roman script) were not attached to their root. Let us take a look at an example below -

It was generally observed that the classifiers and genitive markers were not attached to their root form while writing in Roman. This could be possibly because of the lack of a standardized writing convention in a non-native script like Roman and the identification of a false word boundary by the speakers, which led them to separate the root and the affix in the texts. We did not normalize such instances and in order to annotate such fragments, the 2 new tags were introduced. The reason for not normalzsing texts like these was 2-fold - a) these could actually be an indication towards the way language is processed and word boundaries recognised by the speakers and b) in case there is a variation, it may point towards sociopragmatic usage of separating out certain kinds of 'affixes' from their roots.

All the other tags carry the same meaning as in the universal dependencies tagset. Emojis in the text were marked as Symbol.

2.3 Monolingual Assamese Dataset and Annotation

In addition to the code-mixed annotated dataset that we created, we also acquired monolingual Assamese dataset, prepared as part of Indian Languages Corpora Initiative (ILCI) and made available through Technology Development for Indian Languages (TDIL), Govt. of India. The dataset contains 2 kinds of data original Assamese texts from newspapers, magazines, etc from more than 10 different domains and translated Assamese texts (source language: Hindi) from the two domains of entertainment and agriculture. The total dataset that is currently available consists of 52,000 part-of-speech annotated sentences. However, we use only a small portion of the dataset for this study. The data was annotated using the Bureau of Indian Standards (BIS) tagset that has been declared the national standard for annotating Indian languages data. However, since all other datasets used in the experiments have been annotated with Universal Dependencies tagset, it was necessary that Assamese dataset also uses the same tagset. Since there is no Assamese dataset annotated with Universal Dependencies POS tagset available, we developed a simple mapper to map the tags of BIS tagset to those of Universal Dependencies. Since BIS tagset is

Sl. No.	Category	Label
1.	Noun	NOUN
2.	Proper Noun	PROPN
3.	Pronoun	PRON
4.	Adjective	ADJ
5.	Adverb	ADV
6.	Verb	VERB
7.	Auxiliary	AUX
8.	Adposition	ADP
9.	Subordinating Conjunction	SCONJ
10.	Coordinating Conjunction	CCONJ
11.	Determiner	DET
12.	Interjection	INTJ
13.	Numeral	NUM
14.	Particle	PART
15.	Punctuation	PUNCT
16.	Symbol	SYM
17.	Other	X
18.	Suffix	SUFFIX
19.	Prefix	PREFIX

Table 2: Part-of-Speech Tagset

Takei....	etiya	Raj	da'i	break	**tu**	dilei	hol	aru...
INTJ	now	Raj	brother-NOM	break	**CLF**	give-EMP	happen	and

Now, may rajda give the break and thats it

more fine-grained than the UD tagset, it was a rather simple task to map the tags from BIS to UD tagset. The mapping is given in Table 3.

While for the most part the mapping was quite straightforward and simple to implement, there were a couple of instances where the differing guidelines made the things a little difficult. One was the case of general quantifiers. Generally, quantifiers occur at the position of demonstrative in a syntactic structure and this is probably the reason why quantifiers are classified as determiners and not numerals in UD. However, in the BIS tagset, it is grouped with the numerals. Similarly, BIS tagset do not have determiners as a separate category but they have demonstratives which do not appear in UD. The reasons again seem to be syntactic - since UD is more generally designed for syntactic parsing, the POS categories are accordingly defined. In both these cases, we followed the UD guidelines while mapping since that is the tagset which is being mapped into.

In addition to these, UD does not have echo-word at POS level - it has been included as a morphological feature, which is pretty obvious. Since it was not possible to map this to any POS category in UD, we used a new category called 'suffix' to map echo-word to. It could be argued that it is not a POS category but it is also not meant to be so. It is only a placeholder such that it could be properly handled at the morphemic level. Furthermore, since we are using this category in annotating the social media data also, it also provided some kind of consistency.

Aside from all this, what was surprising was that the Assamese dataset was not annotated with the information about 'classifiers'. Since BIS tagset provides for a category called 'classifier' and Assamese is quite rich in terms of classifiers, this category must have been included. However since it was not present in our dataset, we have not mapped it to any other category. In any case, it does appear in some dataset, like echo-word, it could also be mapped to 'suffix'.

Sl. No.	BIS Category	BIS Tag	UD Category	UD Tag
1.	Common Noun	N_NN	Noun	NOUN
2.	Nloc	N_NST	Noun	NOUN
3.	Proper Noun	N_NNP	Proper Noun	PROPN
4.	Personal Pronoun	PR_PRP	Pronoun	PRON
5.	Reflexive	PR_PRF	Pronoun	PRON
6.	Relative Pronoun	PR_PRL	Pronoun	PRON
7.	Reciprocal	PR_PRC	Pronoun	PRON
8.	Wh-word	PR_PRQ	Pronoun	PRON
9.	Indefinite Pronoun	PR_PRI	Pronoun	PRON
10.	Deictic Demonstrative	DM_DMD	Determiner	DET
11.	Relative Demonstrative	DM_DMR	Determiner	DET
12.	Wh-word Demonstrative	DM_DMQ	Determiner	DET
13.	Indefinite Demonstrative	DM_DMI	Determiner	DET
14.	Main Verb	V_VM	Verb	VERB
15.	Auxiliary	V_VAUX	Auxiliary	AUX
16.	Adjective	JJ	Adjective	ADJ
17.	Adverb	RB	Adverb	ADV
18.	Postposition	PSP	Adposition	ADP
19.	Subordinating Conjunction	CC_CCS	Subordinating Conjunction	SCONJ
20.	Coordinating Conjunction	CC_CCD	Coordinating Conjunction	CCONJ
21.	Default Particle	RP_RPD	Particle	PART
22.	Interjection	RP_INJ	Interjection	INTJ
23.	Intensifier	RP_INTF	Particle	PART
24.	Negation	RP_NEG	Particle	PART
25.	General Quantifier	QT_QTF	Determiner	DET
26.	Cardinal Quantifier	QT_QTC	Numeral	NUM
27.	Ordinal Quantifier	QT_QTO	Numeral	NUM
28.	Punctuation	RD_PUNC	Punctuation	PUNCT
29.	Symbol	RD_SYM	Symbol	SYM
30.	Foreign Word	RD_RDF	Other	X
31.	Unknown	RD_UNK	Other	X
31.	Echo-word	RD_ECH	Suffix	SUFFIX

Table 3: Mapping of BIS Assamese tagset to Universal Dependencies tagset

2.4 Monolingual English Dataset and Annotation

For English, the monolingual annotated dataset was obtained from the dataset provided for CoNLL 2018 shared task. The dataset was annotated using the Universal Dependencies tagset. We used the Universal Dependencies English Web Treebank v2.2, which consists of 16,622 sentences, taken from five genres of web media: weblogs, newsgroups, emails, reviews, and Yahoo! answers. As with the Assamese dataset, we used only a randomly sampled small subset of this dataset for our experiments.

3 Challenges and Issues: A comparison

Both the approaches to processing code-mixed multilingual documents monolingual ensemble approach as well as novel multilingual approach come with their own unique set of challenges and they need to be handled in their own way. We shall discuss some of the challenges that we faced and how we solved those.

3.1 Requirement of helper technologies

The monolingual ensemble approach assumes the availability of the helper technologies for the languages in the text. For our research, these technologies include the following

a Word-level language identification system: It is the first pre-requisite of the monolingual method that the language of the tokens be correctly identified so that they could be processed by the systems of respective languages. For our experiments, we used the system described in (Bora and Kumar, 2018).

b Part-of-Speech taggers: We developed part-of-speech taggers for English as well as Assamese using the monolingual data for the respective languages mentioned in the previous section.

c Transliteration System: Like most of the other Indian languages, a significant proportion of Assamese is written in Roman script over the web. However, the monolingual systems are developed to work on the texts in native script. As such a transliteration module is required to transliterate the roman texts into native script so that the monolingual taggers could process the data. For our experiments, since Roman Assamese transliteration system is not available, we used Roman Bangla transliteration system, which is a very close approximation because of the mostly shared script of the two languages.

The novel multilingual approach, however, only requires that a new part-of-speech tagger be trained for the complete dataset.

3.2 Different Standards and Formats

As we have been seen in the previous section, English and Assamese have used two different 'standards' for part-of-speech annotation of the dataset. In this case, since both the tagsets have been quite standardised and have been in use for a lot of languages, it was a relatively simple task to map those. However, in a lot of different tasks, there have been a large number of different tagsets and annotation schemes, with a glaring lack of a standard, to the extent that every language uses a different annotation scheme. In such a situation, mapping of tagsets such that the tagsets of all the languages in the code-mixed data are same, might become a herculean task and, in fact, may not be completely possible in certain instances.

However, developing a new system using the code-mixed dataset rules out any such requirement of mapping different tagsets for different tasks.

3.3 Error Propagation

It is a commonly known fact that the greater the number of systems involved in a pipeline, greater is the error as the error from one system propagates and multiplies through different stages in the pipeline. As we have seen, the monolingual ensemble approach requires that at least 2 (and sometimes even more) systems work in the pipeline. This is likely to increase the error count. In the following section, we will see the extent to which an ensemble system leads to huge errors in the whole pipeline.

4 Experiments and Discussion

We developed 3 different part-of-speech taggers - Assamese, English and Code-mixed - as part of our experiments. All the 3 taggers were trained on a dataset of approximately 1,700 sentences each. We divide the dataset into train:test ratio of 90:10. The train set is used for training a Linear SVM classifier using 5-fold cross-validation. We tune only C hyperparamter of the classifier and arrive at the best classifier using Grid Search technique. We use scikit-learn library (in Python) for all our experiments. The following set of features gave the best performance for all the three classifiers -

Word-level Features: We used the current word, previous 2 words and next 2 words as features.

Tag-level Features: We used the tags of previous 2 words as features.

Character-level Features: We used the first three characters (prefixes) and last three character (suffixes) as features for training

Boolean Features: In addition to the above features, we also used the following additional features has_hyphen (1 if the word has hyphen in it), is_first / is_second (1 if the word is the first / second word in the sentence), is_last / is_second_last (1 if the word is the last / second last word in the sentence) and is_numeric (if the word is a number).

We will be releasing the dataset and the models trained during the experiments for further research as well as reproducibility of our results

These classifiers were tested in 3 different ways to assess the relative performance of the systems developed using the two different approaches to processing code-mixed data. These are discussed in the following subsections.

4.1 Same train-test dataset

This is the classical testing of the classifiers where we test the classifiers on the dataset of the same language as it was trained on. Thus the classifier trained on Assamese monolingual dataset was tested on Assamese monolingual dataset and so on. The test results set a benchmark to compare the loss of performance when tested on the other datasets. The performance of the classifiers is summarised in Table 4

Train Set	Test Set	Precision	Recall	F1
Assamese	Assamese	0.90	0.90	0.90
English	English	0.88	0.88	0.88
Code-mixed	Code-Mixed	0.85	0.84	0.84

Table 4: Performance of part-of-speech taggers tested on the dataset of same language

As we could see, the classifier for code-mixed data performs the worst. This is not very surprising given the low amount of data that was used for training. However, with similar amount of data, the other 2 classifiers performed comparatively better. This could be attributed to the fact that the monolingual dataset is more consistent and noise-free than the code-mixed data and thus comparatively easier to fit than the code-mixed data. Moreover, it must be noted that in this case, it is not just that the code is mixed; rather the dataset is from social media and contains several other kinds of inconsistencies including non-standard spelling and punctuation, use of emoticons, presence of hyperlinks, etc. As such, the training data required for training a code-mixed classifier is more than that required for monolingual classifier, in order to achieve a comparable performance.

4.2 Train on code-mixed, test on monolingual

In this case, we used the part-of-speech tagger trained on code-mixed dataset to test on both the English as well as Assamese monolingual dataset. A comparative performance of the classifier on both the monolingual datasets as well as the code-mixed dataset is summarised in Table 5

Train Set	Test Set	Precision	Recall	F1
Code-mixed	Assamese	0.64	0.65	0.64
Code-mixed	English	0.67	0.65	0.65

Table 5: Performance of part-of-speech taggers trained on code-mixed dataset and tested on the monolingual dataset

As expected, there is a drop in the performance of the classifier when it is tested on a dataset different from the one it was trained on. In fact, it was not just a different dataset, it was trained on a dataset with a different language and consequently dataset with a large amount of vocabulary not present in the train set. Given the fact that, for a task like part-of-speech tagging, the classifier was not performing at its best, the drop in the performance is reasonable.

4.3 Train on monolingual, test on code-mixed

In this last case, we basically followed the ensemble approach of annotation where we use a pipeline of 4 different systems to annotate the code-mixed test set with part-of-speech information and evaluate it. Figure 1 shows the annotation pipeline.

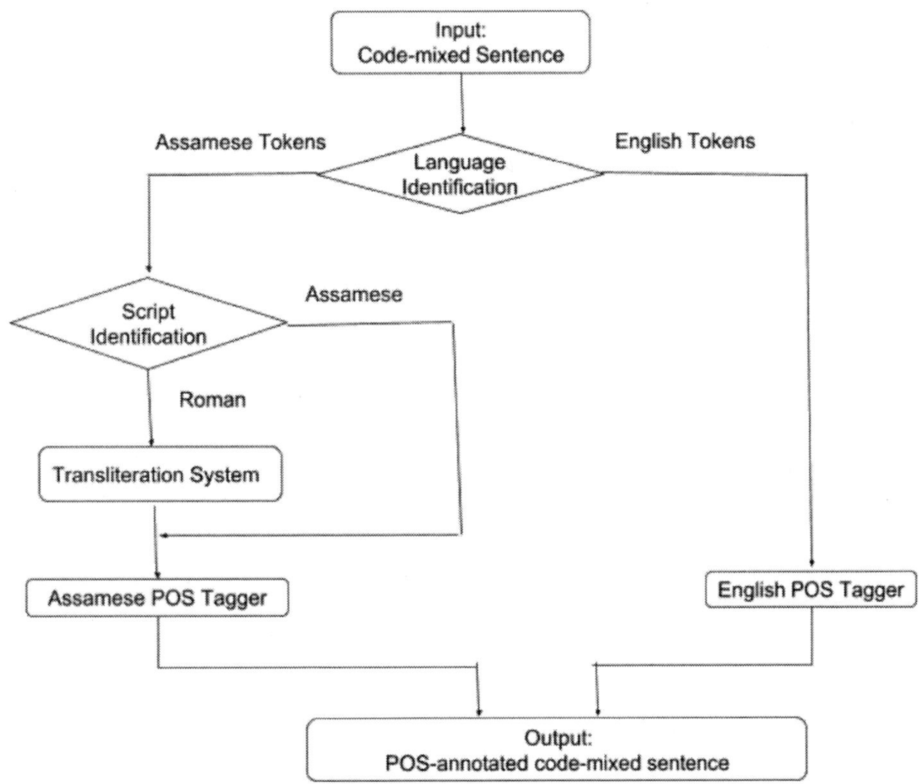

Figure 1: The annotation pipeline for code-mixed data using ensemble approach

In the first step, the test set was annotated with language tags at the word-level. Then the Assamese tokens in Roman were transliterated using Google's transliteration system for English-Bangla pair since there is no transliteration system available for Roman to Assamese. Finally in the last step, depending on whether the token is English or Assamese, the English or Assamese tagger was used to annotate it. If the token was a punctuation or an emoticon, they were marked as punctuation and symbol without using the tagger. The performance of this system vis-a-vis the one trained on the code-mixed data is summarised in Table 6

Train Set	Test Set	Precision	Recall	F1
Code-mixed	Code-mixed	0.85	0.84	0.84
Assamese + English + OT [1]	Code-mixed	0.59	0.50	0.50

Table 6: Performance of part-of-speech taggers tested on code-mixed data

The huge drop in the performance of the classifier is pretty obvious. It is not difficult to guess the reason behind this drop. It is not just the errors made by the part-of-speech classifier but also the errors by the language identification system as well as the transliteration system (the fact that it was not even English-Assamese transliteration system and the data that we transliterated was from social media did not help either) that overall resulted in a performance like this. It would be interesting to explore how the system will perform if we assume that language identification and transliteration systems performed perfectly well. We already have the test set manually annotated with language tags and we are currently in the process of manually transliterating the test set. Once done, we will be able to report on how much the errors in each system of the pipeline add up to. However, despite this, in practical applications, we cannot expect to get manually annotated and transliterated datasets and as such in real-life we expect the system to perform as reported here.

5   Summing Up

In this paper, we have discussed the issues and challenges of using the monolingual ensemble approach over the novel multilingual approach. We argue that, given the number of technologies required for using the ensemble approach, it may not be a practical or even beneficial approach to follow if the required systems are not already available for all the languages in our dataset. On the contrary, if we are building new tools and technologies for any language, it would be highly desirable that such systems are trained on multilingual code-mixed data from the social media for some very obvious reasons. It is quite easy and quick to collect such data. Also our experiments show that training a system on code-mixed data performs relatively well on monolingual data. Moreover, while the overall annotated data required for a comparable performance on code-mixed dataset is more than that required for building a monolingual system, the overall data requirement is actually less than the overall data required for building systems for *all* the languages in the code-mixed dataset.

References

P. Auer. 1995. The pragmatics of code-switching: A sequential approach. In L. Milroy and P. Muysken, editors, *One Speaker, Two Languages: Cross-Disciplinary Perspectives on Code-Switching*, pages 115–135. Cambridge University Press, Cambridge.

U. Barman, A. Das, J. Wagner, and J. Foster. 2014. Code mixing: A challenge for language identification in the language of social media. In *Proceedings of the First Workshop on Computational Approaches to Code Switching*, pages 13–23.

Manas Jyoti Bora and Ritesh Kumar. 2018. Automatic word-level identification of language in assamese english hindi code-mixed data. In *4th Workshop on Indian Language Data and Resources, Proceedings of the Eleventh International Conference on Language Resources and Evaluation (LREC 2018)*, pages 7–12.

M. Cardenas-Claros and N. Isharyanti. 2009. Code-switching and code-mixing in internet chatting: Between 'yes', 'ya', and 'si' a case study. *The JALT Call JOurnal*, 5(3):67–78.

A. Das and B. Gambck. 2014. Identifying languages at the word level in code-mixed indian social media text. In *Proceedings of the 11th International Conference on Natural Language Processing*.

J. John Gumperz. 1964. Hindi-punjabi code-switching in delhi. In *Proceedings of the Ninth International Congress of Linguistics*, The Hague. Mouton.

P. Muysken. 2000. *Bilingual Speech: A Typology of Code-Mixing*. Cambridge University Press, Cambridge.

Carol Myers-Scotton. 1997. *Duelling Languages: Grammatical Structure in Code-Switching*. Clarendon Press, Oxford.

D Nguyen and A. S. Dogruoz. 2013. Word level language identification in online multilingual communication. In *Proceedings of the Conference on Empirical Methods in Natural Language Processing*, pages 857–862.

T. Solorio and Y. Liu. 2008a. Learning to predict code-switching points. In *Proceedings of the Conference on Empirical Methods in Natural Language Processing*, pages 973–981.

T. Solorio and Y. Liu. 2008b. Parts-of-speech tagging for english-spanish code-switched text. In *Proceedings of the Conference on Empirical Methods in Natural Language Processing*, pages 1051–1060.

Y. Vyas, S. Gella, J. Sharma, K. Bali, and M. Choudhury. 2014. Pos tagging of english-hindi code-mixed social media content. In *Proceedings of the Conference on Empirical Methods in Natural Language Processing*, pages 974–979.

Author Index

Association for Computational Linguistics
209 N. Eighth Street
Stroudsburg, Pennsylvania 18360

ISBN 978-1-5108-6907-3